slate

COVER DESIGN BY JESSE MARINOFF REYES
in homage to Reid Miles, repurposing photographs by Paul Cantin, John Carrico, Roman Cho, along with several uncredited promotional images

INTERIOR PAGES DESIGNED BY GRANT ALDEN

Copyright © 2009 by No Depression
All rights reserved
Printed in the United States of America
First edition, 2009

Requests for permission to reproduce material from this work should be sent to:
    Permissions
    University of Texas Press
    P.O. Box 7819
    Austin, TX 78713-7819
    www.utexas.edu/utpress/about/bpermission.html

♾ The paper used in this book meets the minimum requirements of ANSI/NISO Z39.48-1992 (R1997) (Permanence of Paper).

ISBN 978-0-292-71929-3

Library of Congress Control Number: 2008931429

This volume has been printed from camera-ready copy furnished by the author, who assumes full responsibility for its contents.

NO DEPRESSION

the bookazine (whatever that is) #77 • spring 2009

Back when we were a bimonthly magazine, articles mostly were assigned around the release date of record albums. And then, when we were in the tired stretch of being done, often we would discover some barely visible current running through the issue: a particular supporting musician whose name cropped up, an obscure songwriter whose work seemed again to be on lips, maybe simply a mood or a worry which pervaded.

With this, our second bookazine, we sought to direct that process. Sorta. We sent a note to some of our favorite writers asking that they pitch us stories for which they had no other possible home, especially in this era of print contraction. And then we allowed a theme to emerge.

That we sent our note out during the last campaign season meant that, yes, change was in the air. But the change w wanted to write about was not, in the main, political. It was about the transformative power of music. Which is, more or less, what it's always been about, in the end.

Thanks for reading.

— GRANT ALDEN & PETER BLACKSTOCK

DOCK BOGGS ☞ BOUGHT HIS GIBSON BANJO AS A MEANS OF MUSICAL UPWARD MOBILITY. GARNARD KINCER BECAME ITS GUARDIAN FOR A QUARTER-CENTURY, KEEPING IT DOWN TO EARTH.

The first notes sounded flat. Mike Seeger reached halfway up the neck to the first peg, twisting, testing the low string. It wouldn't stay in tune. He shrugged apologetically and started playing again. His fingers worked the banjo effortlessly, even though he said he didn't play these songs much — "Country Blues," "Pretty Polly" — songs that were first picked on this instrument nearly 80 years ago by a Virginia coal miner named Moran Lee "Dock" Boggs. In Seeger's hands, they still sounded natural as thunder.

The strings were thick and wiry. Seeger hadn't changed them since he bought the banjo from Sara Boggs, Dock's widow. "Dock used heavy gauge strings," he said. "I don't play heavy gauge strings very much. But when I play that banjo, it's remarkable. It has a tone that I really associate with Dock's music." He paused. "It's deep."

This was sometime in the spring of 2000. I was in Lexington, Virginia, visiting Mike Seeger because I wanted to see Dock Boggs' banjo. Seeger, the folklorist, music historian and indefatigable apostle of banjo music, was crucial to the rediscovery of Boggs in the early 1960s. He has been the keeper of Boggs' 1928 Gibson Mastertone since Boggs died in Needmore, Virginia, in 1971. It is a fine old instrument, well cared for and, as I found when Seeger passed it to me, heavy in your hands. Through its association with Boggs — and, for that matter, Seeger — it is part of an important lineage in American music.

Boggs is a sort of archetypal Appalachian figure, a rugged man from a rugged place with a craggy, keening voice and a coal train percussiveness in his clawhammer playing. He was never famous, exactly, but the twelve sides he recorded in 1927 and 1929 have endured and been championed and romanticized for their stark, bracing clarity by successive generations of enthusiasts. All of which is reason enough to prize his instrument, as Seeger does.

But my interest in the banjo went beyond Boggs. Because, in fact, he and Seeger are only two of its three owners. For a few decades, between when Boggs quit music and when he took it up again, the Mastertone with the deep thrum was in the possession of a man named Garnard Cheldon Kincer. He made no records, performed no concerts outside the confines of the living room and front porch, and left no legacy of his proprietorship except in memories passed down by his

HERE OL' RATTLER HERE

by JESSE FOX MAYSHARK

children. His claim on history is narrower than Boggs', but in its own way is deep and rich.

Boggs' story is by now well told, most notably in Barry O'Connell's essay "Down A Lonesome Road," which accompanies the Smithsonian Folkways anthology of Boggs' later recordings. But the full narrative of his instrument, the biography of his banjo, puts the mythology of Boggs' life in a context both broader and more specific than the haunted abstractions of his songs. If Seeger makes good on his aim of leaving the banjo in the care of the Smithsonian or some other keeper of cultural records, the legacies it carries with it will include not just one man's music, but the daily rituals of a place and time on the border between one age and the next.

The banjo always came along. On family outings, Garnard would put the instrument in the car first, before letting any of the children climb in. When he worked for a while as a guard at an ammunition plant in Radford, Virginia, it was the only companion he took with him on his five-day sojourns. One day in the 1950s, he was working on the engine of a bus he drove for the family's church. Pushing in the fan belt, he started the motor, which pulled in his arm and took off the last three fingers on his left hand, the fretboard hand, above the middle knuckle. "He let that heal over," said his son, G.C. Kincer Jr., "and he still could take those stubs up there and run them stubs up and down, buddy, and he could pick that banjo as good as anybody you've ever heard. He was right in there with Dock Boggs."

Modern banjos are direct descendants of traditional African string and drum instruments, brought to the New World by slaves. European chroniclers noted them as early as 1678, and in 1781, Thomas Jefferson observed of plantation detainees, "The instrument proper to them is the Banjar, which they brought hither from Africa." White musicians appropriated the banjo and its songs for the blackface minstrel shows that were omnipresent in the 19th century. And from there it spread widely, mixing and mingling with other contemporary forms.

"The way that something that was so black becomes so white, of course, is the fascinating thing," said Philip F. Gura, a professor of literature and culture at the University of North Carolina and co-author (with James F. Bollman) of *America's Instrument: The Banjo In The Nineteenth Century*. "The instrument became very popular in the minstrel shows," he said, "and then in the post-Civil War period, certain white players began to use it for playing sort of more complex music, European-style music."

Soon there were banjo recitals on concert stages, banjo tunes in the parlor repertoire of the leisure class, banjo-guitar clubs on college campuses. And in more rural areas, especially the Scots-Irish communities of the Appalachian mountains, the banjo became a key component of string-band music, working comfortably alongside the fiddle and mandolin.

"The mystery is how much it remained being played among black people, and there's not a lot of evidence for that," Gura said. "The main documentation tends to be about these white virtuosos."

He thinks the decline of black banjo playing was hastened in the early 20th century by the birth of the recording industry, which early on subdivided the marketplace into economic, cultural and geographic niches. Rural white music was "hillbilly"; music by and for black audiences went into the broad, segregated category of "race."

"And race records meant the emergent blues and early jazz, in which you don't find the five-string banjo prevalent," Gura continued. "Whereas the hillbilly stuff continued in that string-band tradition, and that's where you get Charlie Poole, you get the Skillet Lickers, people like that, who are the white purveyors of this older style. By the 1920s, I think because of the recording industry, this instrument now became associated primarily with the white rural music."

This was the cultural landscape that shaped Dock Boggs. He was born in 1898 in West Norton, Virginia, one of the dozens of towns that clattered to life in central Appalachia around that time to serve the industrial nation's hunger for timber and coal. He went to work in coal mines when he was 12 and finally quit 44 years later when his body couldn't take it anymore. In between, he learned to sing, and to play banjo.

Boggs' family was full of musicians. Of his nine brothers and sisters, at least half played banjo, and nearly everyone sang. He took to it easily and, for reasons not hard to appreciate, developed a local reputation, playing at dances and festivals (and once, according to an anecdote he related to Seeger, for gas money so he could drive home across the mountains). But that wasn't enough for him. Coming of age at the dawn of the recording industry, Boggs was part of the first generation to see the possibilities in taking his regional music beyond the boundaries of parties and porches. In a previous era, "professional" music was the stuff made by and for the educated classes, with

Day shift, Mine 4, Haymond, Kentucky, July 6, 1939. Garnard C. Kincer is in the front row, third from the left. Photographs courtesy Sarah L. Cornett-Hagen.

orchestras and concert halls and fancy dress. But the twin advent of records and radio created a medium and an audience for almost any music you could name. Record labels eager for new product and new markets sent scouts into small towns across the country looking for talent. When men from the New York-based Brunswick label came to Norton in 1927, Boggs went for an audition. Offered a contract, he agreed to make the trip to New York to record eight songs. Before he left, he bought a new suit, so he wouldn't look like a country boy.

The instrument he was playing at the time was something Boggs later referred to as a "Silvertone." Mike Seeger thinks he maybe meant "Supertone," because Seeger owns one by that name that looks a lot like the one Boggs is holding in early photographs — a lean body, with an open back and a thin neck. It was something he bought from a mail-order company, a common resource for rural musicians. In the recordings, it is sharp and bright as it follows the melodies of Boggs' vocal lines. (This mirroring, a sort of duet between voice and instrument, was a hallmark of his style.)

After the Brunswick sessions, in the hope of more to come, Boggs decided he wanted to upgrade his relatively cheap accompaniment. About to turn 30, he'd already been in the mines for nearly 20 years, and his encounters with full-time musicians convinced him their line of work was preferable to his. But if he was going to make a living from his music, he figured he'd need the best equipment he could afford. With some of the money from his recording sessions, he bought himself a Gibson.

"These are heavy instruments," Seeger said, looking at the banjo. "There are no heavier." He added, "To me, the Gibson banjo had a supreme balance of volume, cutting quality, and that deep tone."

Gibson had been making banjos since 1918, representing with a few other brands the top end of the market. The Mastertone model Boggs bought was among the most expensive available, probably retailing in the vicinity of $100. Seeger thinks the banjo represented to Boggs the same thing his new suit did — a chance to break out of his inherited life and livelihood, to join the emerging modern world of the 1920s, which was still distant in many ways from the Appalachian hollows that were providing its fuel. Although the music he played came from rural mountain traditions, he was determined to play it on the best commercially produced instrument he could afford.

> "Daddy never had a lesson," Garnard Kincer's daughter Willie Jo said, admiringly. "He wanted to play so bad, he always liked it, and he couldn't play. And one night he went to bed and he dreamed he could play, and he got up the next morning and picked up the banjo and played."
>
> "Had a dream," G.C. repeated.

Boggs never got the opportunities he hoped for. He did record four more songs, using the new banjo, for a regional record company, Lonesome Ace, in 1929. Then the Depression hit, and the market for records slumped. Playing for a living proved unworkable, not least because Boggs' wife, Sara, disapproved of the late nights and hard drinking that seemed inevitably to accompany it. Soon, he went back to the coal mines. He wouldn't record again for 34 years.

"He bought this banjo and wanted to be a professional," Seeger said. "He did that for six months. And it didn't work."

Around the same time, Boggs found it necessary to get out of Norton for other reasons. A complicated feud involving a local lawman named Doc Cox (Boggs' early life was full of complicated feuds) made it seem prudent to decamp just over the hills to Kentucky. It was there, in a mining company town in the mid-1930s, that Dock and Sara Boggs for a time rented out the upstairs rooms of their house to a young Garnard Kincer and his wife, Reba. He was a miner, she was a schoolteacher. In 1936, they had a daughter, Sarah.

Sarah Kincer (now Sarah Hagen) has lived for years in Ashland, Oregon. But as often as she can, she comes back to Eastern Kentucky, which is where I met her by accident one afternoon. We were both visiting the studios of the radio station WMMT, an arm of the Appalshop arts and culture agency in Whitesburg, Kentucky. In the hallway outside the DJ booth, we got to talking about music, and eventually she asked me if I'd heard of Dock Boggs. I nodded enthusiastically, and out came the story of the banjo.

Sarah has in recent years been writing reminiscences of and poetry about a childhood

Garnard Cheldon Kincer and Reba Brooks Adams Kincer, November 1936. Their first daughter was three months old. Photograph by Shorts Studio, Neon, Kentucky.

that even she acknowledges seems like it took place in a different world. She doesn't remember the Boggses — she was too young — but her mother told her that Sara Boggs coddled her during her first year. Sara Boggs was unable to have children — "I think that was a major issue between her and Dock," Seeger said — and apparently even once inquired about adopting the Kincers' infant daughter. The offer was politely refused. "Mama said she felt so sad for Sara when she tearfully told her she could have anything she owned, but not her baby," Sarah remembers.

But Sarah, like her siblings, does remember the banjo. Because long after the Boggses exited the Kincers' family life, the banjo remained.

How that happened depends on whom you ask. Seeger said Dock Boggs told him he finally quit playing music to appease Sara and put his drinking behind him. As proof of his commitment to "living right," he got rid of the banjo, pawning it to his upstairs neighbor, a man he'd been teaching to play. The Kincer children grew up with a slightly different version of this story.

"Dock Boggs came by," G.C. Kincer said with a grin, "and he was gonna get drunk. He was $16 shy or something like that. I'm not sure about the figure, but that's close. Dad gave him $16 and he left his banjo with him."

Whatever the circumstances of the exchange, it marked the beginning of the second phase of the banjo's life. The man it passed to had as many ambitions as Boggs, although none of them involved making money from music — and, like Boggs', they remained largely unrealized. Garnard Kincer, in his children's recollections, was a man of sly wit, sincere devotion to family and church, and big ideas that never quite panned out. He also had a devoted amateur's love of the banjo, which produced a trove of family legends.

"They only lived over Dock Boggs a year or two," G.C. said when I talked to him and

Willie Jo, shortly after meeting Sarah, their older sister. "That's when Dad got to meet him, and that's when Dad took up the banjo, and that's when he taught Dad. Dock Boggs was a claw-picker, and so was Dad. I can remember seeing his fingers doing that — " He makes a claw with the thumb and last two fingers of his right hand.

By the time Willie Jo and G.C. were born, their father was playing every single day, maybe even more than he worked. "Dad didn't work a lot," G.C. said fondly. "He 'saved himself.' This is what he told my mother. And one day she said, 'Garnard, every time I talk about you getting a job, you're all the time saying that you're saving yourself. What are you saving yourself for?' And he said, 'In case you get sick, and I have to work.'"

Nevertheless, he was up early every morning to wake his children. Taking the Mastertone, he'd stand at the foot of the stairs and play "Here Ol' Rattler Here," a traditional picking tune that served as the family's "Reveille." The instrument was an object of magic and fascination for the children, and some amount of horseplay. Willie Jo and G.C. remembered riding it hobby-horse style through the house with little concern that the neck, held firmly in place by an internal trust rod, might snap right off.

Willie Jo still lives in the family home, in the small community of Haymond. It's just a fifteen-minute drive from Whitesburg (itself a town of just 1,500), but obscure enough that the receptionist at Whitesburg city hall had to consult with another clerk to give directions. Haymond still has the look of a company town — a long row of nearly identical two-story frame houses

The Kincer family, South Fork Pound, Virginia, fall 1946, shortly before the birth of G.C. Sarah is on the right, in the front row.

lined up between a narrow road and a creek. When the terrain permits, which isn't often, there are houses on the other side of the road too, reaching up a steep hill in small clusters. One of those clusters includes the Kincer home, a small house with green siding that makes it seem less weathered than some of its neighbors. The coal company that built the town is, like many in Eastern Kentucky, long gone, bought out or shut down or merged with one of the increasingly large conglomerates that control most of what remains of the region's mining industry. The only evidence of Haymond's founding history is a small Chevron processing plant on the town's outskirts, and the caravans of coal trucks that still rumble down the narrow two-lane highway, rattling the windows and doors of homes built right at the edge of the road.

Garnard Kincer imagined himself as the owner of some of those trucks. "He always envisioned making it big in the coal business," G.C. said. "He had this huge dream that any day he was gonna hit it." He and a friend invested in a "dog hole," the kind of mine you could work with a small crew and a few hauling trucks. "They would go get 'em a coal lease," G.C. continued. "They'd scrape and scrape and scrape and scrape and go up there and face that coal up. And they'd go in there and dig that coal. But what he found out was, it was a lot easier to dig that coal on paper than it was to dig it out of that mountain."

"Lordy," Willie Jo added, laughing, "if they had had all the money they made on paper…"

Then there's the story of Buddy the bulldog. The family pet liked to lie at Garnard's feet while he played banjo, sometimes wagging his tail. He also had a tendency to stray, spending days or weeks chasing females in heat.

"We knew every time he went out that he wasn't coming back, 'cause he'd likely got killed or something," Willie Jo says. "Well, this time, he'd been gone for about a month, wasn't it? And Daddy said, 'Well, Buddy's gone. Buddy-dog's gone for sure this time. He's not comin' home.' So it was one night we were sitting around. Daddy would play the banjo. And he was sitting there, playing, 'Here ol' rattler here, here ol' rattler here, come ol' rattler from the barn, here ol' rattler here.'"

"And he'd pat his foot when he played, like this," G.C. said, tapping his right foot.

"Well," Willie Jo continued, "when he'd pat his foot, he heard this — " She thumped the table twice. "And Mother told him, 'Play that song again.' Daddy played it again, pat that foot, and they heard this — " She thumped the table again. "Well, we lived in this house, and it was an old shack-like house, just an old shack that was thrown together. And the floor of the back bedroom was right next to the ground, there was just a little opening under. And Daddy was sitting there and patting his foot, and he kept playing that song over and over, and the more he played it, the louder these got," meaning the thumps.

"That dog," she concluded, "had got hurt and come home and crawled up under that floor under that back bedroom, and got hung and couldn't get out. And he'd been up there for we don't know how long." Garnard, who loved the dog, ripped up the floorboards to get him out.

"But the banjo is what found the dog," G.C. said.

"The banjo found the dog," Willie Jo agreed, "by playing 'Here Ol' Rattler Here.'"

The Kincer children grew up knowing the banjo's history, and Dock Boggs' name, but as far as they're concerned, it only ever had one true owner. For more than 25 years, it was like an extension of their father himself. Until the day Dock Boggs came to get it back.

Boggs told Mike Seeger he had been wanting to play again since his retirement, and he'd never forgotten the Gibson Mastertone, the instrument that had made him feel like a real musician. So he tracked down the man he'd left it with, and paid him a visit.

That day in the living room, G.C. Kincer said, his father used the banjo to teach his children one more lesson. Boggs had brought with him several hundred dollars — the exact amount is fuzzy in Kincer lore — and offered it to Garnard Kincer. Garnard refused all except what he had paid Boggs for the banjo, years before. "You've got to understand," G.C. said, "it was not a matter of the value of a banjo between Dock and Dad. It was a matter of the value of a man's word.

"We needed money," he continued. "You know how bad we needed it. We were poor. And Dad said, 'I'll take the $16 that you pawned it for.' He said the lesson he taught us was priceless. He knew some of us would think the banjo was priceless. He said it was a better lesson to teach his children to be a man of your word. And here was his word.

"We didn't want it to go," G.C. said, adding with some lingering defiance, "That banjo was more the Kincer banjo than it ever was Dock Boggs'."

Mike Seeger went on the road periodically with Boggs in the 1960s. He has stories about taking him to Ann Arbor, Michigan, where Dock sat at cafeteria tables swapping tales with students; about being refused service at a roadhouse in Tennessee because the two of them were accompanying Elizabeth Cotten and Bessie Jones; about Dock's ongoing struggle to reconcile hard living with hard moral convictions. The banjo in some ways relates to all of that, the straddling of eras and the grinding of cultural tectonic plates. It is at once an instrument of tradition and modernity, of the sitting room and the recording studio.

"That's an industrial banjo," Seeger said, by which he means it was mass-produced and commercially marketed, unlike the generations of homemade instruments that preceded it. "And so was the previous banjo he owned. And it was owned by one of the guys from what I consider the climax of pre-commercial music."

Boggs, of course, wasn't trying to play pre-commercial music. He wanted to be commercial. And he halfway succeeded. If he hadn't managed to get into a studio, his songs would have been lost like countless, nameless others. He was on the edge between something disappearing and something not quite formed, and his records are documents of dislocation. Like Gardnard Kincer in his company house with his dreams of wealth just ahead, Boggs saw a world coming at him

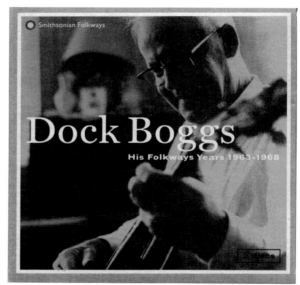

What Dock Boggs did with the banjo: The most recent Smithsonian Folkways summary of his later work. The cover photograph was taken by Dan Seeger in 1963.

and tried to get a purchase on it. For Boggs, the banjo was a ticket out that never quite paid off, at least not until it was too late to really matter. For Garnard Kincer, who maybe knew he wasn't really going anywhere, it was something like the opposite: a totem of his place and time that let him merely enjoy being where he was.

Garnard Kincer never owned another banjo, even though he lived until 1978. He bought a broken one once, but he never got around to fixing it up. His son Mack played, and occasionally

He wanted to be commercial. And he halfway succeeded.

Garnard would pick up Mack's instrument and strum a little. But his children recalled that he'd always set it back down quickly. Like Dock Boggs, he thought nothing else sounded quite right.

"He was heartbroken I think, when that banjo went," Willie Jo said softly. But the Kincers avowed no hard feelings. Dock Boggs was Dock Boggs, after all, and a deal was a deal. Still, if the banjo is to pass into the national official record somehow, they think it should be with its history intact — its whole history.

"You know…" G.C. said, "if that happens, I'd like to see the real credit given to the right guy, and that's my dad. For preserving it, for having it there when he came back to get it. I'd like for one time in his life that he gets some credit. That'd be good. Because he deserves it, because he did take care of it, he kept it.

"Now," he said, "both of those guys are dead."

"They're playing banjos together in heaven," Willie Jo said.

G.C. nodded and laughed, and added, "Except Dock might have a little hard time explaining what he used that $16 for."

Jesse Fox Mayshark lives in New York City, where there are more banjo players than you'd think. In a note accompanying photographs lent for this article, Sarah L. Cornett-Hagen — Garnard Kincer's first-born — writes, "It is my heartfelt desire to bring the banjo back home to Letcher County, to be showcased in a museum in Whitesburg, KY."

mississippi yearning

THE VOICES OF PANOLA COUNTY RAISE IN PRAISE, and HOPE FOR MORE

by EDD HURT

The Como Mamas. Photograph by Matt Rogers.

"IT ALL STARTED with us trying to help Angela's son," says Della Daniels. Angela Taylor, Daniels' younger sister, lives in Como, Mississippi, but she attends church in nearby Looxahoma, at West Looxahoma Church of Christ. "Him and some little friends of his at school, they was makin' a CD and doing some rapping," Daniels continues. "They had named themselves Scorpio, and when Angela called me over, I put it in the CD and listened to it, and I couldn't believe it. It actually sound like a record that was already out."

An energetic and assertive person, Della Daniels tells her story of what sparked the sixteen spirituals which make up *Como Now: The Voices Of Panola Co., Mississippi* in a way that makes it clear she should have been listed as the project's co-producer. That's not to discredit the initiative of Michael Reilly, the 30-year-old aural documentarian who set up equipment in a non-air-conditioned church on July 22, 2006, and captured Daniels and her friends, family and acquaintances rendering "It's Alright" and "Talk With Jesus" and other staples of southern (mostly Baptist) spiritual song. Reilly made the journey from New York to Mississippi's Hill Country, but Daniels did the footwork in Como and Senatobia, buttonholed a few people, and brought in the talent. Released in August 2008 on Daptone, *Como Now* came about, then, from the desire for worldly success, as noble a motive for singing as any other.

Della, who is in her late 50s and lived in Memphis for a quarter-century before moving back to Como in 1997 ("It begun to get so scary, living up there; I started having a lot of break-ins in my home," she remembers), got on the case for Scorpio. "I went to the library and read a few books on how to get your song published, and we had a CD machine which would cut — you know, make some more CDs, and we made some," she says. "I sent them to some of the addresses that was out of the books. No luck."

Daniels actually had a sort of music-business pedigree, since her grandfather — a blues guitarist named Miles Pratcher — had recorded songs with the singer Fred McDowell (and others) back in 1959 for folklorist Alan Lomax, who swung through northeast Mississippi in September of that year. Some members of Daniels' extended family had been receiving small checks for those recordings. In search of someone who might listen to the Scorpio CD, Daniels took it upon herself to call the Alan Lomax Archive and got on the phone with Bertram Lyons, who was managing the archives. Lyons knew about the 1959 Miles Pratcher recordings (one of them was "I'm Gonna Live Anyhow 'Till I Die", featuring Pratcher on guitar). Daniels was interested in making a connection for her nephew's

Irene Stevenson. Photograph by Matt Rogers.

homemade rap project, and she probably mentioned, in passing, that she sang, just like virtually everyone she knew in Panola County.

Acting on the tip from Lyons, who had gotten Scorpio's CD and was curious about the relationship between blues and gospel in 1959 and hip-hop in 2004, Reilly called Daniels. A Houston, Texas, native who had gotten the folk-music bug while a student at the University of Texas, Reilly was planning a road trip from New York to Texas, which he wanted to document. "That was the first time we rolled through there," Reilly says. "We met the Como Mamas that time; they weren't called that then."

Meanwhile, Scorpio had split, but Daniels still had plans to get her nephew's music noticed by someone outside of Mississippi. When Reilly hit town, she decided to figure out a way to keep him there long enough to make that happen. "We were trying to think of a way to hold Michael here," she says. "And while they were here, we told 'em, said, 'Hey, we sing,' and he said, 'Y'all do?' And we said, 'Yeah, we sing in church.'"

As Reilly laughs, "I thought I was interviewing them, but it turns out they were interviewing me." Della and Angela began to sing some numbers for Reilly, and called over their cousin Ester Mae Smith, who had copies of the Miles Pratcher recordings. She showed up quickly. "That was kinda odd, because Ester usually make up excuses not to show up when you call," Daniels recalls.

Suitably impressed by what he heard, Reilly made plans to return to town the following summer. "I recorded the Como Mamas [Daniels, Taylor and Smith] then, which is something I really hope to get out soon," he says. "It's a whole 'nother world of stuff." (Since the recording of

Como Now in July 2006, Reilly has returned to Panola County again and recorded several hours of material by the Mamas and other singers in the area. He currently does production and post-production sound and mixing for films and television shows.)

The a cappella performances on *Como Now* come out of a tradition of poverty, from singers accustomed to making their way without pianos or guitars. As Daniels says, "It has been really hard to keep musicians at churches." Too, the Mt. Mariah CME Church, where Reilly conducted the sessions, lacks funds in a serious way. That's why Daniels decided to ask potential participants in the sessions to pay up-front for the chance to make their voices heard.

"I told [Reilly], 'I know a lot of peoples who sing, but since we're trying to finish our fellowship hall, what I would really like to do is charge maybe $25 to anyone who comes, and maybe help raise a little money for the church.'" This begs the question of what would have happened had someone paid and then had their performance left off the final product, but Daniels reveals a deeper motive for her actions.

"A lot of the people here, when they have a family member die, they want to bring them home to Mt. Mariah," she says. "But most of them don't belong to the church, so we are the ones who are havin' to try to keep the church up, keep the cemetery up." The fairly nominal donation would have gone to finishing the fellowship hall, it seems, but Daniels, perhaps inadvertently, reveals what might be called resentment. Of course, the split between the expectation of a service and the reality of who pays for providing it is hardly unique to Como in the pinched, scared post-Bush era.

What makes the Como story compelling is that we're talking about music. And not just any music, but gospel, which is supposed to be about the works of the Lord, Jesus' sacrifice for humanity, and notions of selfless action that hang like big, fluffy clouds over a crowded world. The singing on *Como Now* is inspired about as often as you'd expect from a reasonably controlled sampling of talent in a small Mississippi county. Irene Stevenson's performance of "If It Had Not Been For Jesus" might stand as the collection's most aesthetically pleasing moment on a record all about singing as accompaniment to everyday life, but everyday life almost certainly trumps — makes idle, one might say — ideas of aesthetics.

Rev. Robert Walker. Photograph by Matt Rogers.

As you might imagine, no one wanted to pay to sing at the Mt. Mariah CME Church on July 22, 2006. "Some of them said they had their own recording studios, and they'd already recorded some songs for themselves," Daniels says of her efforts to round up the singers she knew from Como and environs. It's the information age, and nearly everyone has access to technology that Alan Lomax might have envied, even in a small Mississippi community where many people still don't have internet access. (Daniels made up flyers that showed the Daptone logo and put them in mailboxes and into peoples' hands — a distinctly old-fashioned method that, amazingly, didn't include either e-mail or taking out an ad in the local paper.)

There was, in fact, quite a pool of local talent, and Daniels proved herself an exemplary, persistent organizer and psychologist in convincing some of them to participate. Now in their 80s, Brother and Sister Walker had toured with big-time gospel acts such as the Soul Stirrers and the Swan Silvertones, and are highly regarded in the area. "I had to talk to them for a long time," Daniels says. "I mean, they didn't want to do it. They had already made a recording of their own, and they told me that someone they knew from California had been down a week or two before and they had actually given this person some of their CDs."

Brother and Sister Walker made it out to the session with their son, Rev. Robert Walker, a bassist and singer in his early 50s who had grown up playing in a group he'd put together with his brother and four sisters. "I took my mother and father to meet [Reilly] on their recording session, and I considered myself a by-stander," he says. "The peoples in the area know me for singin' and preachin', and they kept asking me to do a song on there. I finally gave in."

Robert Walker's song, "I Can't Afford To Let My Savior Down," demonstrates an approach to solo singing that is some distance from the brassy, extroverted Como Mamas tracks. His voice is hushed and his sense of time tends to the rubato, with cannily employed silences. It's a remarkable performance. As Reilly says, "He has somewhat more vulnerability in his voice, which really opened [the collection] up and changes it. Before

Brother and Sister Walker.
Photograph by Matt Rogers.

the release, I played him the recording, and he kinda saw it for the first time and heard himself in a different light."

It could be that Robert Walker felt, and feels, somewhat superfluous in comparison to his talented parents, who turn "I Can See So Much" into a bravura display of call-and-response singing. Done in a slow-drag tempo, "I Can See" juxtaposes Raymond's gruff vocal with Joella's lighter tone. Appropriately for a couple who have been married for over 50 years, they sound inextricably bound to each other — one soul with two distinct but intertwined manifestations.

Many of the other performances demonstrate the power of friendship and blood ties. On the sublime "Talk With Jesus," the Jones Sisters make it clear they've been influenced by pop singing. Brittany, Dorothy, Tara, Tambra and Tawanda are all in their 20s, and their tart, sprightly harmonies amount to a kind of minimalist pop blues, as if a Phil Spector session from 1962 had been stripped of its Wall of Sound and transplanted to Mississippi in the present age, complete with non-secular subject matter.

This amounts to a semi-pro approach to music that seems both out of time and influenced by the world outside. Daniels is aware of the gulf between those who record and collect performances such as these and the ordinary people who make them. "I think Mike considered what my grandfather and them were singing more like folk music," she says. "I think he considered gospel to be more like folk music, because everybody just about sing the same songs in gospel. In our culture it's gospel. It may be folk music to them."

The *Como Now* songs are presented, no doubt, as folk music, and appear on a New York label known mainly for the retro-soul stylings of Sharon Jones & the Dap-Kings, who evoke the James Brown revue circa 1967. Certainly, the time and effort spent in procuring vintage equipment to produce Sharon Jones' old-fashioned soul sound makes for a nice contrast with the way the Como tracks were made: Reilly used a couple of stereo microphones, a small pre-amp and compressor, and a portable DAT machine. "They hardly even noticed the mikes were there," he says.

Daniels might dismiss the idea that her singing will be perceived as folk music, but it certainly qualifies as such. It's music made by people who have been singing the old songs for most of their lives and will, most likely, continue to sing them, although not the same way every time. After all, folk music quietly mutates, and Reilly says he's gotten some very different takes on the same material in later trips to Como.

In the end, it's not the quality of the singing that means the most when you're listening to *Como Now*, although it's mostly quite good, if a bit indifferent to pitch at times. Nor is it the opposition between folk expression and professional extrapolation. What matters is the way the record urges you to ask the unanswerable question: Why do people make music? Michael Reilly believes that most of the Como singers would jump at the chance to turn pro. "A lot of them had those hopes early on and had resolved to have a regular job and sing on Sundays, but now this has re-stoked that aspiration."

So: Aspiration, whether it's worldly or in the service of the Lord. As Daniels says, "We perceived Michael Reilly as an honest person, and this has made us willing to go ahead and take a chance, because unless you have money to put behind what you're tryin' do to, a lot of people are gonna die with they talent."

A Tennessean raised in the Cumberland Presbyterian Church, Edd Hurt has often attempted to sing in church, but he mostly listens, which is probably a service to his fellow worshipers. He does admire great singing, not to mention singing that comes directly from the heart, and has spent a lot of time figuring out exactly what separates the two.

by *JOE NICK PATOSKI*

SQUEEZE

Why the accordion is

photographs by JOHN CARRICO

PLAY
the national instrument of Texas

At ten o'clock on a Friday evening, about twenty people occupied the rickety tables inside Salute International, a small bar on the St. Mary's club strip just north of downtown San Antonio. Among them were Traci Lamar, an accordionist from Austin, and her guitar-playing sister La Conni Hancock, who perform together with their mother as the Texana Dames, along with retro swamp pop bandleader Larry Lange, also from Austin, a few of their friends, and a handful of Mexican-American regulars. All were Steve Jordan fans, and most of them knew he was dying of cancer.

Over the course of four 45-minute sets, the diminutive figure with an eyepatch and a snap brim cap performed what amounted to a semi-private concert in the corner by the window of the dimly-lit club. Flanked by two taller sons playing bass and timbales and singing harmonies with a drummer behind them, *el maestro* delivered what amounted to a crash course in how edgy a box player can get with a small three-row Hohner Corona diatonic button accordion.

He played the basics, running through polkas, setting the beat, then flitting in and around the beat by throwing trills, diminished fifths, and sudden key shifts when the ear least expected it on top of the basic melody and rhythm. He played with the same casual, comfortable command that John Coltrane blew the sax or Miles Davis his trumpet, as if the small instrument were an appendage (come to think of it, when he wasn't holding his squeezebox, he looked like something less than a whole person), using it as a means to take a seasoned listener to places he didn't know the accordion could go.

El Parche, as Esteban "Steve" Jordan is also known, stretched the music way beyond the traditional framework of conjunto, a sound built upon polkas, along with waltzes, boleros, huapangos, and other traditional Mexican tempos, that has been associated with Texas-Mexicans since the early 20th century. Jordan first mastered conjunto as a teenager more than fifty years ago and was a pioneer who incorporated the *cumbia* and other pan-Latin rhythms into the mix.

"Volver, Volver," the sentimental Mexican anthem of longing and the desire to return, was punched-up into a *cumbia*, with Jordan picking up a drumstick to add a few beats of his own on the timbales and cowbells. He did Cannonball Adderley right on his version of "Mercy, Mercy, Mercy," one of the few songs he sang in English that night (two others were Buck Owens' "Together Again" and the San Antonio brown-eyed soul classic "Ain't No Big Thing" by Little Jr. Jesse & the Teardrops), although it's doubtful that Cannonball wrote the tune thinking a cat with an eyepatch working a button accordion, squeaking and squealing all the way, could sound as rich and full-bodied as Adderley's soul-jazz sax. He pushed the envelope all night playing polkas, cumbias, salsa, blues, soul, country, and Afro-Cuban jazz.

Witnessing Steve Jordan one last time reinforced a notion that's been running around in my head for most of my life: The accordion is the National Instrument of Texas.

Esteban Jordan (overleaf, at right), onstage at the H&H Ballroom, outside of Austin, Texas, August 2008.

Around the same time Steve Jordan was performing his first polkitas in a *salon de baile* (Spanish for dancehall), I was a 6-year-old kid in Fort Worth laboring with a larger piano accordion, struggling mightily to push and pull the big bellows while trying to press the notes to a European waltz on the piano keys with my tiny fingers. I didn't get too far, eventually giving up music lessons to play Little League, although many years later as an adult I bought a Hohner Corona and learned "Viva Seguin" from a neighbor who showed me which buttons to push.

I never could get the sound out of my head. Full-bodied and melodious, the accordion was a whole orchestra in a single musical instrument. I was already hard-wired through my Lithuanian and Greek roots. The music of both cultures included variations of a squeezebox. Then I got lucky when my family moved to Texas when I was 2. I've been having accordion epiphanies ever since. The Texas accordion is not some museum piece that symbolizes an extinct musical style whose time has come and gone. Nor is it a folk instrument meant to be worshipped reverently while sitting and listening attentively, as if in a Vienna parlor. Forget the Lawrence Welk/Myron Floren stereotypes, the Weird Al Yankovic associations, and the Playing Accordion Is Not A Crime bumper stickers, which are about as funny as the name of that northern California band Those Darn Accordions. The Texas accordion is a loud, funky, greasy tool meant to get people dancing, or at least shaking their hips. It packs such a cross-cultural appeal that Gianfranco "John" Gabbanelli left his family's accordion factory in Italy in 1961 to set up

an extinct musical style whose time has come and gone.

Gabbanelli USA in Houston, where he designed new models for a broad customer base hungry for innovation.

Today, Gabbanelli USA offers diatonic button accordions, the kind favored by Tex-Mex conjuntos, which are played like a harmonica, the bellows changing notes when they are pushed or pulled; chromatic accordions, which can change keys like a fancy chromatic harmonica and have a particularly large following among Colombian *vallento* players; piano accordions, with piano keys rather than buttons on the right keyboard, which are bigger, fuller-sounding, and most often associated with European polka bands and orchestras; the *norteño* models preferred by Mexican regional *grupos* who rule the airwaves and pack the dancehalls across northern Mexico into southern Texas; and the Cajun King, the small, lightweight diatonic model with a single row of ten buttons and four exposed stops on the right side and six bass buttons on the left, tailored for white Cajuns and black Creoles, most of whom reside between New Orleans and Houston.

But the instrument is only half of the equation. It really comes down to who's playing it.

Leonardo "Flaco" Jimenez was the first to demonstrate the difference a player could make, courtesy of Doug Sahm and his 1973 album *Doug Sahm And Band*, the star-studded Jerry Wexler production for Atlantic Records that was supposed to be Doug's post-Sir Douglas Quintet return to the pop charts. But even the presence of a vocally inspired Bob Dylan, along with Dr. John, David Fathead Newman and other heavy friends couldn't push Doug into the top ten. The album definitely enhanced Doug's street cred in Austin, where he had moved after growing up in San Antonio and spending the late 1960s in San Francisco, since it led to Willie Nelson and Jerry Wexler getting together.

The real surprise of the album was Flaco Jimenez, whose accordion fills embellished "Wallflower," the Dylan original from his countrified *Self Portrait* period, and put some dance kick into Doug's cover of "Is Anybody Going To San Antone," the album's not-so-successful first single. Flaco's accordion sounded like no accordion had before. When I leaned close enough to the speakers, I could hear his fingertips hitting the buttons so hard, audible taps accompanied the notes. That inspired me to jump down the rabbit hole.

Doug was borrowing a sound he grew up with. His first national hit with the Sir Douglas Quintet, "She's About A Mover," released in 1965, was promoted as the latest sound out of the British Invasion even though the band was really from San Antonio and cranking out a Tex-Mex polka backbeat, with Augie Meyer's Vox organ providing the backfills instead of an accordion. Doug didn't stop with Flaco. He mastered the bajo sexto twelve-string guitar that accompanies

---

At left, Esteban Jordan at work. Above, Flaco Jimenez at the Austin Music Awards, 1995.

the accordion in both conjunto and norteño music, which is specific to northern Mexico, although it shares many of conjunto's characteristics; and he wrote numerous regional pop classics, including "Nuevo Laredo" and "Soy Chicano," which became a much-covered Chicano anthem. He spent the last ten years of his life touring and recording with Meyer, Jimenez, and Freddy Fender as the Texas Tornados.

Even though he'd been to New York to help Sir Doug make an album, Flaco was making his *dinero* playing for Spanish-speaking audiences around San Antonio, fixing accordions on the side. It was about that time that I started going to see *El Gran Flaco Jimenez y Su Conjunto* at the Rockin' M, a metal-sided dancehall out in the country on the Lockhart Highway, a half hour from downtown Austin.

Think of conjunto as Mexican music Texanized, performed by a small combo rather than a big band. The word literally means "group" in Spanish, but in south Texas, the description distinguishes a small combo from a big band and defines a sound built on the polka, appropriated from Czechs, Germans, Poles, and Slovenians who settled in central and south Texas in the 19th century and brought their music and instruments with them. Texas-Mexicans appropriated the polka and embraced it as their own, pepping it up into a bouncy, infectious rhythm that can be as primal and mesmerizing as reggae or trance music, given its simple repetitive elements.

Flaco's father, Santiago Jimenez, credited as one of the fathers of conjunto, showed up at several Rockin' M dances and told stories about learning polkas by hanging outside German and Czech dances when he was growing up, picking up the melodies, then reinterpreting them. Conjunto loosened the sometimes truculent, slow-drag rope wrapped around polka's neck that had given the sound a bad name, and transformed traditional European dances into something new and completely different. Don Santiago complemented the stylings of the other father of conjunto, Narciso Martinez, a lean, wizened figure from La Paloma, a settlement west of Brownsville in the Rio Grande Valley, 200 miles south of San Antonio. Narciso was such a prodigy as a young man that when he recorded for Bluebird Records in the 1930s, he made records under his own name and under the pseudonyms of the Polski Kwartet and Louisiana Pete so that various recordings could be sold to record buyers partial to Polish, Cajun, and Creole music. To Narciso, it was all pretty much the same.

Fans of Tejano big bands known as *orquestas*, which catered to a more sophisticated, assimilated audience, typically looked down on conjuntos as cantina music – cruder, more primitive, more country than their R&B and jazz proclivities, more Mexican than Texan. By the 1970s, Tejano *orquestas* featured horns, organs and synthesizers in place of an accordion. But when Tejano exploded and almost outgrew its audience in the early 1990s, largely through the successes of the late Selena Quintanilla, the band La Mafia, and Emilio Navaira, it suddenly became vogue to add accordion as a retro thing.

Unlike Tejano, conjunto was a self-contained music subculture less assimilated into the "general market," as the gringo pop world was known. The scene was pretty much confined to south Texas and wherever migrant farm workers traveled to pick crops — east to Florida, north to Michigan and Minnesota, west to California and Washington state — with San Antonio its

performed by a small combo rather than a big band.

capital. Austin had a small conjunto scene, although it was no San Anto. Still, it was close enough for a steady parade of stars to play *bailes* in halls such as the Rockin' M, including Mingo Saldivar, Agapito Zuniga (El Escorpion de Corpus), Valerio Longoria, Tony De La Rosa, and Cuatitos Cantu, a conjunto featuring dwarf twin brothers, each born with six fingers on their hands, who played matching accordions.

Every so often, battle dances were staged, pitting the accordionists against each other in "shootouts," where they tried to outdazzle one another. Flaco might have been the superior stylist (he's the Chuck Berry of conjunto, its modern godfather and standard-bearer), and Agapito might have played with more seasoning, but whenever Mingo Saldivar was involved, the outcome was a foregone conclusion. "Pingo" Mingo, the Conjunto Cowboy, was the consummate showman, playing his accordion behind his back, over his head, and between his legs while he kept

dancing, a sure-fire way to win the crowd's approval. Mingo would go on to achieve fame in Mexico, where Texas conjuntos rarely ventured, by interpreting "Ring Of Fire" and other Johnny Cash classics into Spanish.

Flaco went on to take conjunto worldwide. His accordion fronted a small combo of drums, bass, and bajo sexto, which, when strummed, provided the backbeat and counterpoint to the accordion lead. Lyrics were beside the point, although phrases such as "*borracho* number one" and "*el pantalon* Blue Jean" were easy to decipher, and the song "In Heaven There Is No Beer" was sung in English, German, and Spanish.

"Viva Seguin," a song composed by Flaco's father, Don Santiago, captured the essence. The instrumental was as much a

Flaco Jimenez at Club 71, Austin, Texas, 1999. The percussionist at far right is, yes, Matthew McConaughey.

march as a polka, the beat strutting and strident, with the bass holding down the bottom while the bajo bounced off the squeezebox. Flaco gave his Hohner button box a workout, hitting a flurry of high notes you didn't know were there with a flash of his fingers followed by third, fifth, and seventh chords packed with sweet-sour aftertones. His long, elegant fingers danced constantly atop the buttons, prompting hundreds of pairs of feet to dance along on the expansive floor in front of the band, sliding and stepping, heads bobbing along up and down, as if on a merry-go-round, only with more energy and enthusiasm.

Flaco demonstrated that an accordion could be as flashy as a guitar when he took a lead. He also showed how the accordion could be an instrument of romance and sentiment by trilling notes to a ballad or sticking to full chords. It wasn't just polkas, either. Flaco was just as schooled in playing waltzes, redovas, huapangos, and the cumbia, which was increasingly gaining favor in all kinds of Latin music being *hecho en los Estados Unidos.*

For several months' worth of gigs at the Rockin' M, Flaco's conjunto included Ry Cooder, who was learning bajo sexto so he record an album featuring Flaco called *Chicken Skin Music,* and take Flaco on the road with him. The Rockin' M crowd was oblivious to Cooder, politely applauding whenever Flaco introduced the gringo in his band to his audience, saving their cheers for whenever Flaco announced "mas musica." Following Cooder, Flaco went on to play and record with Peter Rowan, David Lindley, Dwight Yoakam, Emmylou Harris, Bryan Ferry, the Clash, Willie Nelson, Buck Owens, Los Lobos, Linda Ronstadt, the Mavericks, and the Rolling Stones, eventually becoming a charter member of the Texas Tornados.

Flaco eventually led to *El Parche,* Steve Jordan, the virtuoso accordionist who played like Jimi Hendrix and ate acid like popcorn. Or so the legend went. I was turned on to Steve by Mike Buck, the original drummer for the Fabulous Thunderbirds, Robert Ealey & the Five Careless Lovers, and the Leroi Brothers. It was around the same time Mike was turning me on to Li'l Millet's swamp pop jewel "Rich Woman" (thirty years before Robert Plant and Alison Krauss covered it), the turban-wearing

Little Joe Hernandez (left) with Esteban Jordan, August 2008.

Count Rockin' Sidney's "You Ain't Nothin' But Fine," "She's My Morning Coffee," and "Tell Me," along with the complete works of Cookie & the Cupcakes.

Even among those esteemed outsiders, Steve Jordan stood out. Proof was the A side of a 45 rpm single, his conjunto interpretation of the Vanilla Fudge's psychedelic version of the Supremes' 1966 Motown hit "You Keep Me Hangin On." Steve's version was just as spacey and freeform as the Motown version was tight – *acordeon psicodelico,* according to the description on the label. The vocals were compelling, pained and tortured like the Fudge's. The instrumentation was otherworldly, his accordion drenched in reverb, distortion, and feedback. Considering Jordan had also covered the Coasters' "Yakety-Yak" *en español,* written a smoldering blues shuffle called "Squeeze Box Man" as well as the passionate Chicano anthem "Canto El Pueblo," and spent time on the west coast playing guitar with Afro-Cuban jazz percussionist Willie Bobo, a psychedelic polka wasn't so unusual.

While under the Mexican influence, I was also heading east, mostly to chase whatever it was that made Clifton Chenier & His Red Hot Louisiana Band the most exciting live band I'd ever witnessed, churning up enough energy and collective passion to easily levitate a room while going full tilt for four hours without pause. Clifton's brother Cleveland played rubboard, scraping a corrugated metal vest he wore around his shoulders with two handfuls of beer can openers, which added a layer of rattlesnake rhythm to an already primal funk. Between his instrument, its sound, and the way he played the rubboard, Cleveland was the band's sexual focus, the perfect counterpart to Clifton, who was always way out front, working the piano keys of his giant-sized Paolo Soprani accordion while he dueled with Blind John Hart's searing sax or added a second rhythm guitar chunk to Little Buck Senegal's groove.

The music was built upon waltzes and two-steps — the basic elements of Cajun music — which Clifton could ably articulate. But the repertoire also covered slow, deep blues, popping rhythm and blues jump, boogie-woogie, and driving Fats Domino-inspired rock 'n' roll, as played by a black band.

Those add-ons separated zydeco from Cajun and, ultimately, Clifton from everyone else. His fingerwork was exquisite and elementary at the same time (visualize Ray Charles playing piano on "What'd I Say," only sideways while holding up his instrument) in front of a big band that could have been directed by Brother Ray or Joe Scott, the arranger and bandleader behind Bobby Blue Bland, Little Junior Parker and all those other great Duke-Peacock uptown blues recordings. Or, as Clifton once explained in his raspy voice with typical understatement, "I put a little rock into the French music."

He'd already been around the block, having had a hit R&B single for Specialty Records in 1955 with a mambo-fied cover in French of a Professor Longhair tune, "Ay Tete Fille (Hey, Little Girl)," and cutting tracks for the Chess blues label. More recently, he'd been recording for Chris Strachwitz's folk music label Arhoolie, making records in a single day that were earthy, but fell short in fully conveying the electric excitement of Clifton in his element, playing live.

Even the syrupy sentiment expressed in songs such as "Don't Let The Green Grass Fool You" and "What's Good For The Goose (Is Good For The Gander)" sounded honest with the

Clifton Chenier

accordion in the lead. The same went for "Deacon Jones," a traditional "under-the-counter" song featuring blue lyrics, which became another joyous stomp instead of just another dirty song when the accordion was cranking; and for that old warhorse, "Jole Blon."

Clifton was the real deal, down to the way he signed his autographs "Your fren." He knew he was good, too. Every night, he donned a crown for a few songs to show one and all who the King of Zydeco was. And though the band was identified as Louisianan and was based in Lafayette, Clifton was part Texan, having lived in Houston, the Los Angeles of zydeco, where country boys leaving the fields could find work. The Texas-Louisiana border at the Sabine River was just a line on the map to music-making Creoles such as Clifton, anyway. On any given Saturday night, at least two Catholic Church parish halls in Houston were throwing zydeco la-las, where the beer was cheap, the flirting was in French, and the gumbo was home-cooked.

Still, I wanted to know more about the source-point farther east where Community Coffee, frozen daiquiri drive-through, platters of shrimp and mudbugs, Louisiana Hot Pepper Sauce, and all the good music came from. My guide was Leon Eagleson, the blackest white man I've ever known; he ran OK Records next door to the original Antone's nightclub in downtown Austin and functioned as Clifton's booking agent for Austin. Whenever Clifton played Austin, which was practically once a month in the mid-1970s, the band's first stop was in the back of Leon's store, where drinking, smoking and shooting craps was standard operating procedure. It was a wonderful window to Clifton's band, who as a whole impressed me as possessing more raw power than the Rolling Stones and more inspiration than Bruce Springsteen.

Like Antone's owner Clifford Antone, Leon hailed from the Golden Triangle, the far southeast corner of Texas. He took me home first to introduce me to the joys of Cajun music in its element at the Rodair Club in Port Acres, as performed by Allen Thibodeaux and the French Ramblers, and to the exotic pleasures of zydeco in its element at Our Mother of Mercy Catholic Church parish hall in Port Arthur, courtesy of Good Rockin' Dopsie & the Twisters, who got down and dirty in front of a black Creole dance crowd.

Seeing Clifton Chenier in a concert hall or an Austin club or the New Orleans jazz festival was one thing. Experiencing Clifton at the Ten Acre Club out in a darkened field somewhere between Lafayette and Lake Charles on a Sunday night was transcendent. There, he played real folk music for real Creole folks — his people — fueling a burning rhythm that summoned sweat and steam from every single body squeezed into the wooden building on cinder blocks.

A double bill with Lightnin' Hopkins at Jay's Lounge and Cockpit, a roadhouse somewhere near Cankton, Louisiana, frequented by a younger white crowd, may have been the wildest show I've survived. Jay's was both a dancehall and a rooster cockfighting venue (the loser wound up in the gumbo), located far enough away from civilization to be wide open, if not necessarily legal. On this weeknight, there was such anticipation that before the doors were even opened, a window near the stage was smashed and half the crowd waiting outside poured in, crawling through glass shards to get in for free.

Clifton played as if that happened all the time.

started following Good Rockin' Dopsie & the Twisters, too, who were a rawer, cruder version of Clifton's band. Dopsie played diatonic button accordion, a far smaller accordion than Clifton's. His rubboard player, Mr. Shorty, played one-handed with a single bent fork instead of two hands full of church keys. He was nonetheless cool enough to prompt Blind John Hart and his saxophone to leave Clifton.

Zydeco had a crowded pantheon of greats — characters such as big John Delafose, Wilfred Chavis, Nathan & the Zydeco Cha-Chas, and ultimately Boozoo Chavis, the man behind 1953's

and half the crowd waiting outside poured in, crawling through glass shards...

"Paper In My Shoe," considered the first zydeco hit record. Boozoo never paid much mind to music while Clifton rose to the top and went international, because Boozoo was busy raising horses at his place in Dog Hill near Lake Charles, Louisiana. But in the 1980s, he picked up where he left off and immediately established himself as the visionary primitive, wearing a cowboy hat and an apron to keep the sweat off his belly while working a small single-row, ten-button, Cajun model accordion, the notes primal and redundant enough to whip the crowd into a dervish.

With Leon guiding, we found straight-up Cajun music at a Saturday morning dance at Fred's Bearkat Lounge in Basile, Louisiana, broadcast live on the local AM radio with drinks all around; at another Saturday morning dance down the road in Opelousas that was broadcast on the radio; at the Savoy Music Center in Eunice, where whiskey was produced and a impromptu jam broke out when a fiddler friend of owner Marc Savoy walked in while Savoy was showing one of the Cajun accordions he built; and at a dance that evening near Opelousas where Savoy played with the Balfa Brothers.

We futilely searched for Nathan Abshire, perhaps the finest Cajun accordionist of the moment, in his hometown of Basile. Turns out Nathan was passed out drunk from too many Pearls at 3 p.m., according to his grandson, who was busy trying to learn the chords to ZZ Top's "La Grange" on a guitar.

Boozoo Chavis. Photograph by Barbara Roberds.

Back in Texas, white boys were getting in on the rebirth of the accordion cool. Ponty Bone, a beatnik accordionist from San Antonio who played a big keyboard box, added the secret sauce to the Joe Ely Band, the only west Texas rock 'n' roll outfit since the Bobby Fuller Four that really mattered. Augie Meyer, Sir Doug's sidekick, sometimes played a small keyboard squeezebox when he fronted his own Western Head Band, which he used on his regional sung-in-Spanglish record, "Hey Baby, Ke-Pa-So."

But it was an art student from North Texas State University in Denton named Carl Finch who reinvented the central and eastern European polka, thought to be beyond salvation. With Carl on a small piano key box, his band, Brave Combo, launched "Nuclear Polka" in 1979, selling schmaltz, corn, and cheese by reinterpreting "I Can See For Miles" by the Who, the Doors'

"People Are Strange," and Jimi Hendrix's "Purple Haze" as polkas (eventually embracing "Louie, Louie" as a cha-cha and "Theme From Mission Impossible" as a cumbia), and signing communications "polkatively yours." They managed to insinuate themselves into Dallas' and Austin's nascent punk and new wave scenes (there is nothing quite like a bunch of alt types flapping their arms and squatting as they do the Chicken Dance), then eventually crossed over to ethnic audiences, playing Czech, German, Slovenian, Polish, and conjunto music to crowds raised on the sounds. Brave Combo passed.

The accordion craze peaked somewhere around 1985 when Weird Al became a star and the former Count Rockin' Sidney, now just plain Rockin' Sidney of Lake Charles, Louisiana, reinvented himself as a zydeco player and hit the jackpot with an unlikely novelty song called "My Toot Toot." The tune became a pop hit, a country hit, and a million-seller, then a rare ethnic crossover, inspiring numerous cover versions in several languages, not the least of which was Steve Jordan's Tejano version about "mi linda Toot Toot."

It should've ended there. Or when Clifton Chenier died in 1987, or certainly by the time John Gabbanelli and Narciso Martinez passed away, if not back when the Texas Tornados broke up, and the Rockin' M closed. But even when the Vrazels Polka Band Farewell Tour 2008 wrapped up, Texas accordion didn't stop.

Brave Combo at the Kerrville Folk Festival, 1999.

John Gabbanelli's business grew big enough to open the first Gabbanelli showroom and distribution center before he died in 2003. With John's son, Michael, and his wife, Ella, at the helm, Gabbanelli USA has continued to expand its American (and Texas) presence.

Brave Combo has become institutionally hip, playing at David Byrne's wedding, recording with Tiny Tim, and lionized as cartoon figures on the TV program "The Simpsons" and in Harvey Pekar's *American Splendor* comic book. They are annual headliners at West Fest in the north central Texas town of West, which celebrates its rich Czech heritage over Labor Day weekend, and they play the National Polka Festival in Ennis, Texas, and Wurstfest in New Braunfels, Texas, which in effect makes them the new Myron Floren. They have also inspired a cover band in Holland called Strange Combo and a tribute album by an Italian band, cementing their place as leaders of the alternative polka scene.

Max Baca y Los Texmaniaca, at H & H Ballroom, August 2008.

Brave Combo's pan-accordion approach got the attention of a Polish kid from Saginaw, Michigan, named Bradley Jaye Williams who moved to Austin in 1993. Williams could play four different kinds of accordions, and in Austin, he had plenty of reasons to play them all. He started up his own conjunto, Los Pinkys, with Isidro Samilpa; a Cajun band, the Gulf Coast Playboys, with fiddler Ralph White from the Bad Livers; and the Polkasonics, his Polish-American combo. Lately, Williams has been doing shows with Flaco Jimenez.

Carl Finch recently told the tale of a Wisconsin kid considered the genius accordionist of the Slovenian scene in the Upper Midwest who's moving to Texas to get closer to the real deal. Steve Jordan had changed his way of thinking about his instrument, although the kid doesn't speak a lick of Spanish. But that didn't stop him from making pilgrimages to San Antonio's Salute International bar twice a year. Now he's all in.

Zydeco has grown bigger than ever with a new generation of stars, including Geno Delafose, C.J. Chenier, Terence Simien, Brian Terry, Beau Jocque, and Young Dopsie. They are just as likely to embrace hip-hop influences as their elders once infused blues and R&B into their repertoire. The French la-la lives. The kids got it. The quickest ticket overseas was playing your granddaddy's music, not ZZ Top's "La Grange."

Similarly, Chris Rybak, the Accordion Cowboy who is the son of Czech bandleader Leroy Rybak, has brought new life to Tex-Czech polka, just as Steve Riley and a slew of younger Cajuns have done the same for Cajun chanky-chank music. One of Riley's Mamou Playboys, Peter Schwarz, now fiddles with Charles Thibodeaux (whose cousin owned the Rodair Club back in the Golden Triangle) in the Austin Cajun Aces, which also includes former Leroi Brothers frontman Steve Doerr.

Of all the Texas accordion styles, conjunto's future is brightest. The Guadalupe Cultural Arts Center and the San Antonio Parks & Recreation Department sponsor *tallers*, or accordion schools, where kids and adults can learn squeezebox from the maestros who define it. Conjunto's most articulate scholar, Juan Tejeda, lectures about conjunto music and its culture at Palo Alto College. Joel Guzman gives Latinology performance-lessons with his wife Sarah Fox, collectively known as Aztex, while frequently pairing up with Joe Ely; an album of their collaboration, *Live Cactus*, was issued in 2008.

San Antonio continues hosting the Tejano Conjunto Music Festival in May and the International Accordion Festival in October, and claims the only conjunto radio station in the nation, KEDA-AM, Radio Jalapeno.

But it has been in Houston, at the annual Accordion Kings and Queens concert, where the change is most evident. For the past two years, the sponsoring Texas Folklife Resources has held the Big Squeeze contest, a Future Kings and Queens competition, with area contest winners going to Houston to compete for a cash award and studio time. The contest has been dominated by young Mexican-Americans brandishing Gabbannelli models as flashy and colorful as any rock 'n' roll guitar. One entrant performed while doing knee drops, a la James Brown. A first-year finalist, A.J. Castillo, explored new fusion sounds by mixing what he called "smooth jazz" into his polkitas and cumbias. The second Big Squeeze winner, 16-year-old John Ramirez of Houston, dressed like a pachuco with his fedora and modified zoot suit, working a squeezebox that when extended looked like an American flag. None struck me as the next Steve Jordan or Flaco Jimenez, but who knows? The music was *puro* accordion — nowhere but Texas accordion — meaning there was plenty of room to explore, plenty of room to make more of the instrument that made them.

Steve Jordan.

Those kids came to mind a lot while watching Steve Jordan one last time at Salute International. Steve had made the most of his instrument, if not necessarily of his gifts. I'd seen him play at the Rockin' M in front of *tejanos*; witnessed his crossover to gringo audiences in Austin on the night Esteban and Rio Jordan opened for Doug Sahm at Soap Creek Saloon while the whole band was tripping on acid, I later found out; and lobbied to get him in the David Byrne movie *True Stories*. I became so smitten that I couldn't see the obstinate, self-immolating person behind the artist. He was his own worst enemy, so good he'd break your heart.

And now, 30 years later, he was on his way out the door. I'd lost track of Esteban in the

if not necessarily of his gifts.

mid-1990s, somewhere between the Rio Grande Valley and Phoenix, where he was making obscure albums for obscure labels, playing all the instruments himself, and impulsively canceling interviews with journalists that his then-wife/manager had set up. I'd heard he'd shown up unadvertised to play one of the Conjunto Festivals in San Antonio, and I know he refused to allow John Dyer to use a photograph that John took of Steve for John's book *Conjunto*.

A fundraiser held for him by hepcats outside of Austin had been hyped with a YouTube video of Steve sitting in with Carlos Santana and Jerry Garcia out in San Francisco. When I watched it, it was plain to see he was too strange for Cali rock royalty. It was a marked contrast to the small gathering at Salute International who knew exactly what they were seeing and hearing.

The last time I saw El Parche, he was snapping his accordion into its case, pausing to take a break. I walked out the door and into the thick, humid air hanging over San Antonio, my boots clipping on wet pavement, my head full of sounds made by bellows and reeds, going gently with a spring in my step, into what remained of a very good night.

Joe Nick Patoski is the author of Willie Nelson: An Epic Life, *and writes for* The Texas Observer *and* Garden and Gun. *He was a contributing editor to* No Depression.

FIRST BASS

BOB MOORE HAS WITNESSED AND MADE MUSIC HISTORY HOLDING DOWN THE BOTTOM END FOR NASHVILLE'S STUDIO A-TEAM

BY RICH KIENZLE • PHOTOGRAPH BY DAVID WILDS

"PRACTICE! ONE HOUR!"

When 17-year-old Bobby Loyce Moore, the bass player in Paul Howard's Arkansas Cotton Pickers, heard that order through his hotel room door, he did as commanded: spent a solid hour running scales on his instrument. Fiddler Roddy Bristol, who'd taken an interest in his musical development, got him started and if the scales tapered off too soon, Bristol would be back rapping on the door. The dividends proved huge. Moore called it "a real good experience, because I got into playin' some jazz and faster things you have to think about, rather than just go out and play 'You Are My Sunshine.'"

At 76, Bob Moore looks back on a career that paralleled Nashville's metamorphosis into a worldwide recording center, where he helped create some of American music's most enduring hits. "In those days, a bass player was a comedian in the band. I was something new; I was a player, not a comedian," he asserts. True enough. For the most part, baggy-pants hijinks (think Speck Rhodes with Porter Wagoner) was the norm for country bassists in the 1940s and '50s. Moore, a charter member of Nashville's original studio A-Team and, with an estimated 17,000

sessions, its most recorded bassist, redefined the instrument's role in country much as Jimmy Blanton redefined jazz bass with Duke Ellington's Orchestra. Along the way, he helped to raise the level of Nashville's musical discourse.

His session work transcended genre, from the raw music of Little Jimmy Dickens to late '50s Elvis rockers and landmark Nashville Sound recordings to most of Roy Orbison's quintessential songs (which he also produced). Moore's own moment in the sun came in 1961 with his visionary hit instrumental, "Mexico." During his peak years, Moore worked bluegrass dates, accompanied Chet Atkins on an album with Arthur Fiedler & the Boston Pops and Brook Benton on "Rainy Night In Georgia," and did rock sessions with artists including Bob Dylan, Simon & Garfunkel, and Moby Grape.

Like the music, Moore himself was a product of Nashville. "I never knew my father," he admits. Sidney Moore took a linotype job in Paterson, New Jersey, six months after his first son was born. Sidney's wife Nellie, again pregnant, went with him, while Bobby remained with her mother, Minnie Johnson, at her East Nashville home. His musical fascination bloomed early. Minnie listened to the Grand Ole Opry each week, and the toddler's baby teeth scarred her upright Victrola, where he'd hang on the edge of the console, watching the 78-rpm discs spin.

Minnie and her daughter Ruth worked full-time. With Bobby too young for school, a woman named Zona Robinson provided day care, and her sons, Billy and Floyd, became his closest friends. Aware of his family's modest means, in 1941, 9-year-old Moore trekked downtown to Fifth and

Bob Moore (overleaf) at home in Franklin, Tennessee. Above, with Little Jimmy Dickens. At right, a studio portrait as a made man in Nashville. Vintage photographs courtesy Kittra Moore.

Photo by FORSHEE

Broadway on Saturdays to shine shoes for a nickel. After the Opry relocated to the Ryman Auditorium in 1943, he hung around the backstage door, where musicians and officials befriended him, occasionally inviting him inside.

Moore and his friends delved into music. The Robinsons had guitars; Bob, who played baritone horn in the school band, spied an unused upright bass in the music room and got permission to take the instrument home, providing he returned it daily. The trio practiced at the Robinson home and dutifully lugged the instrument to and from school. Moore taught himself, but during Saturday shoe-shining at the Ryman, he threw musical questions at customer Jack Drake, bassist with Ernest Tubb's Texas Troubadours. "Jack was always kind," he recalls. "I'd ask him something and he'd show me. Jack didn't play any wrong notes, but all he had to play was Ernest Tubb's notes, which is very simple. But Jack had a way of pullin' a string that got a better sound out of a bass than anybody else down there. I mimicked him and it built my right hand."

The Eagle Rangers, a Sons Of The Pioneers-inspired outfit, became the musical outlet for Moore and the Robinson brothers, with future Hank Williams Drifting Cowboy Jerry Rivers playing fiddle. In 1946, the group performed in rural areas outside Nashville and on WGNS radio in Murfreesboro with singer Bob Jennings. Two summer vacations spent backing up Opry blackface comics Jamup & Honey on their tent show tours further honed Moore's stage skills. A 1948 move from Nashville to his mother's New Jersey home lasted only until the Eagle Rangers, booked in South Jersey, visited him. He was soon back in Tennessee.

Bob Moore (back right) playing bass in the tents with Jamup and Honey.

His timing was perfect. At the Opry, Paul Howard and his progressive western swing band the Arkansas Cotton Pickers, sick of stilted musical policies hostile to their progressive sound, quit to try their luck on Bob Wills' turf: the dancehalls of Texas, Arkansas and Oklahoma. Moore, a longtime western swing fan, became the band's new bassist, calling the gig "the prestige of the eons to me, because he was known to have the hottest band there was." A January 1949 Howard session for King Records in Cincinnati became Moore's first actual studio experience.

Unfortunately, with western swing's popularity in decline, the bandleader started missing paydays. One of his guitarists, Nashville native Robert "Jabo" Arrington, Moore's closest friend within the band, quit. Back home, Arrington formed a band for Opry newcomer Little Jimmy Dickens, hiring Moore on bass and ex-Eagle Ranger Floyd Robinson on guitar. When they recorded "A-Sleepin' At The Foot Of The Bed" at Castle Studio in October 1950 (Arrington and future A-Teamer Grady Martin played twin lead guitars), it became the first top-10 country hit to feature Bob Moore's bass.

teachin' me my playing language." — Bob Moore

Newly married when he left Dickens in early '51, Moore spent six months in Houston backing Curly Fox and Texas Ruby before he and wife Betty, expecting their first child, moved to her parents' New Jersey home. Finding musical work scarce there, Bob returned alone to Nashville. Mom Upchurch's boarding house on Boscobel Street, popular with struggling musicians, was home base. His roommate was Hank Garland, famed for his guitar solo on Red Foley's hit "Sugarfoot Rag" and obsessed with mastering jazz.

Monday through Friday, Moore awoke at 4 a.m. to accompany Flatt & Scruggs on their live, 15-minute WSM show, one of eight back-to-back weekday programs hosted by Opry stars. Moore landed several more of these at $3 a pop per day (roughly $25 in 2008 dollars). He occasionally made more by filling in as the star if a singer no-showed. WSM became a classroom for Moore, who hung around for "Noontime Neighbors." Broadcast from Studio C, the daily program blended talk with pop music from WSM's orchestra, led by station music director Owen Bradley, who became Moore's mentor. "He would always say, 'Come on over here, Bobby. Let me show ya.' I'd go over to the piano with him, and he'd lay his ten fingers out on the keyboard and say, 'Now look what happens when I move just this one finger.' He got me watchin' the arithmetic of it. He knew what I could do, and had his part teachin' me my playing language."

Moore's growing family was with him by the time he joined Red Foley's band in 1953. (He and Linda would have two sons and a daughter. R. Stevie Moore has pursued a singular musical agenda, mostly from his New Jersey home studio. Linda played bass in the 1980s country band Calamity Jane.) Foley, a Decca recording artist, had been an Opry star since 1946, but he was depressed over his wife's suicide, and quit to host the new Ozark Jubilee, an Opry-styled radio-TV program from Springfield, Missouri. Moore, working between Nashville and Springfield, found the weekly commute — nearly a thousand miles — burning him out. "I was not in Nashville. I wanted to come back, and it must have showed."

Bradley noted Moore's restiveness at a 1954 Foley session at Castle Studio. At the time, Bradley wore four other hats: Decca country A&R man Paul Cohen's assistant, Decca artist, session musician, and leader of a popular 15-piece orchestra playing Count Basie-flavored swing for dancers at upscale venues around town. After the session, he offered Moore a spot in his band. "I told him, 'I can't make a livin' on that big band,'" Moore recalls. "He said, 'Well, in about six months, Paul Cohen is gonna make me head of the Nashville office [Bradley succeeded Cohen in 1958]. If you can handle that, I'll get you another session or two to help you out, but after I take control, with you workin' on my big band, you'll have all my [session] work.' So that started me, and from then on I was straight ahead."

Playing in Bradley's band deepened Moore's musical range. "I needed to go to college, and I got it right there," he says. He also learned the realities of jazz versus mainstream tastes. "Owen said, 'The public don't like [but] one thing and that's the melody.' He'd say, 'Play me a run,' and you'd play him some kind of a run and he'd say, 'Now sing it back to me,' and you couldn't do it. Then he'd say, 'You are my sunshine…could you sing that back? That's what the public likes!'"

In 1955, with Castle set to close, Bradley bought an old house on 16th Avenue South, built a new studio inside, and added a metal Quonset hut for film projects. Interior remodeling accidentally left the hut with such superb acoustics that "the Quonset hut turned out to be the big cheese," Moore says. That remained so even after RCA opened their famous studio complex in 1958.

Columbia's Don Law, Capitol's Ken Nelson and RCA's Steve Sholes had Moore on their first-call list, leading to his charter membership in Nashville's original A-Team. Aside from Moore, the core group included Bradley and his younger brother, guitarist Harold Bradley. On guitar were Moore's friends Hank Garland and Grady Martin, along with Chet Atkins and rhythm guitar specialist Ray Edenton. Drummer Buddy Harman, a former Carl Smith sideman, used to work with Moore at Nashville's Rainbow Room. "We played dinner music for the early crowd, and then played stripper music for the later drunks," Moore laughs.

Pianists included the iconic Floyd Cramer and Pig Robbins. Boots Randolph and his tenor

Mohair-era Bob Moore, between takes.

sax arrived in the late '50s. The Jordanaires, the Anita Kerr singers and soprano vocalist Millie Kirkham were there from the start. While fiddle and steel were briefly out of vogue, early A-Team fiddlers included Dale Potter and Tommy Jackson; the early steel guitarists were Jerry Byrd, pedal steel pioneer Bud Isaacs and Pete Drake. As session work increased to a constant level, this group of musicians developed into a musical SWAT team, capable of creating cohesive arrangements on the fly and improvising clever musical hooks that enhanced Nashville recordings of all genres.

It all came not a moment too soon. To a Nashville gobsmacked by the havoc rock 'n' roll wreaked upon country record sales in 1956, producers felt they needed a new paradigm. Bradley at Decca, RCA's Chet Atkins (whose path from studio guitarist to A&R assistant to producer paralleled Bradley's), and Capitol's Ken Nelson, a former Chicago pop singer, aimed to expand country's appeal with records acceptable to the core audience but also to pop record buyers, for whom the big-band era was a recent memory. It wasn't a new idea. At Decca, Bradley and Paul Cohen occasionally used vocal ensembles, popular during the big-band years, behind Foley and Ernest Tubb in the late '40s – particularly the Anita Kerr Singers, who worked at WSM. Eddy Arnold's 1954 #1 ballad "I Really Don't Want To Know" featured heavy background vocals. The post-Elvis approach replaced fiddles and steel with vocal harmonies.

In 1956, Nelson used the Jordanaires, who routinely moved between sacred and secular, on Sonny James' "Young Love" and Ferlin Husky's "Gone," their softer, pop-flavored harmonies the inverse of their earlier full-tilt doo-wopping on Presley's first raucous RCA hits. Atkins adapted

rockabilly. We thought we were doin' country music..." — *Bob Moore*

the formula to Jim Reeves in early '57, resulting in "Four Walls," his first crossover hit, copied by other producers.

Moore was present on dozens of other hits using this concept, which earned the sobriquet the Nashville Sound. Among them were Reeves' "He'll Have To Go," Don Gibson's "Sea Of Heartbreak," and Patsy Cline's "I Fall To Pieces" and "Crazy." "'Crazy' is not country in anybody's book," Moore says. "But start that record and listen to it, and it's just a good, clean, not overdone pop record." A-Teamers, he adds, had a credo: "Get in there and learn the damn [song]. If you want to be successful, get your job done and do it well, and that's the truth. The guys settin' in the control room, they're writin' your check, so you know damn well you better deliver, but you're doin' it for them. Back in those days, it was *surely* for them. Their name got on the record and yours didn't!"

Some producers used certain A-Teamers exclusively. In one year, Moore played on 300 sessions for Mercury. "That just kinda happened, through friendship," he says, "hangin' out or gettin' one hit record and [producers] sayin', 'Oh, we gotta have him, he made a hit!' People, their superstitions come out real quick, you know." But Moore also had an intuitive ability to guide singers, providing musical cues to keep them in meter (a challenge even for some great vocalists). It evolved from cues he gave the meter-challenged Dickens onstage in 1950 into more subtle promptings for others. "I got to listenin' during a song to how [singers] would react to different things. Elvis'd always look around [at] me, and wink. And it was just — something that helped them to get back in comfortably without even knowin' it."

Bob Moore (white shirt) conducting a Monument session with Roy Orbison (at right).

As they helped Nashville triumph in the face of rock, Moore and his colleagues, paradoxically, worked sessions with rockers signed to major labels hoping for their own Elvis: Ronnie Self, Johnny Carroll, Johnny Burnette and Janis Martin among many. "We never thought about it," he admits. "I still can't tell the difference between country and rockabilly. We thought we were doin' country music, then later on, it got defined as rockabilly." Moore, Garland, Randolph and other A-Teamers accompanied Presley on his 1958-62 Nashville sessions and onstage at his 1961 Hawaii concert.

A 1959 session with singer Billy Grammer, signed to the new, Baltimore-based Monument label, provided Moore another opportunity when he heard label owner Fred Foster mention that one of his two partners wanted out. A week later, Moore left Baltimore owning 37 percent of Monument. Grammer's hit "Gotta Travel On" was a strong start, but Roy Orbison's pop successes such as "Only The Lonely" and "Blue Bayou," with Moore and the A-Team creating the glossy accompaniment, truly established Monument. Moore, however, kept his ownership stake

"The setup in the Quonset hut...there was nothin' between me and [Charlie Rich's]

a closely guarded secret. "I didn't want to be part-owner of a label and workin' for RCA, havin' them sayin', 'Aw shit man, you know about all we're doin' over here.'"

Sheer happenstance, he says, shaped some hits. At the 1960 Marty Robbins session that yielded his relaxed, bluesy ballad "Don't Worry," Grady Martin was soloing on a six-string bass guitar when a sudden malfunction in either his amp or the mixing board (depending on who one talks to) distorted his sound into what's now called fuzztone. "I'm sittin', watchin' and hearin' every bit of this and playin' at the same time. And that just came up right in the middle of a take. Once we heard it, the guys in the control room were scared we's gonna stop, and they come up to the window and was givin' 'keep goin!' signals. And that was it! Grady is not a player that would play the exact same thing twice in a row. He can follow a program but that is not what he intended. But immediately, when he heard that, and somehow kept goin', he made what he played fit that sound. That's God-given."

During a tour of Mexico with Foley in 1953, a huge, out-of-tune Mariachi band burned into Moore's memory. He developed an idea for that sound. In 1961, while recording instrumentals for Monument as Bob Moore and his Orchestra, he attached that idea to Boudleaux Bryant's instrumental "Mexico," with local trumpeters Karl Garvin and Bill McIlhiney playing the slightly dissonant harmonies. "I was on vacation and started hearin' it on the car radio," he says. "So I called back to our office and they said, 'We been tryin' to find you, because you gotta come back home and go on a promo tour. That damn thing's hittin'!'" "Mexico," which peaked at #7 on the *Billboard* Hot 100 in October 1961, is a point of pride for Moore, one that almost certainly inspired Herb Alpert's phenomenally successful Tijuana Brass concept. (Moore and Foster eventually parted ways over some of Foster's business moves, though they reconciled years later.)

When a day's sessions ended, A-Teamers often continued the music with jazz sessions at Jimmy Hyde's Carousel Club in Printer's Alley. They began when Garland and Moore, whose bass heroes included jazzmen Oscar Pettiford and Stan Kenton Orchestra sideman Eddie Safranski, jammed at the club while rooming at Mom Upchurch's. "That brought business in," he says, "and every guitar player in town started comin' down. Hank was blowin' them away. They were drinkin' Jimmy Hyde's booze and payin' their money. [From] Belle Meade Country Club, rich young stockbrokers started comin', and their out-of-town guests. Within a year or two, you couldn't get in the place."

Some out-of-towners were jazz luminaries. "Stan Kenton come in one night...the greatest thrill of my life. Called me over to his table, complimented me, shoot! I was in big time then!"

The A-Team, Moore asserts, was an organic unit, changing constantly as musicians came and went. Some lacked the temperament, couldn't handle the workload or music business politics. Atkins, Randolph, Ray Stevens and Floyd Cramer became successful solo artists. New blood came from musicians who'd worked their way up the hierarchy. "They called them the B-Teamers for a while. Some got to be A-Teamers later on. [Guitarist] Pete Wade's one, [guitarist] Billy Sanford's another, [bassist] Junior Husky was another one." Guitarist/bassist/harmonica player Charlie McCoy came in the same way.

Sessions were lucrative for A-Teamers. Moore owned and piloted his own planes; in the

left hand except the flat beside me where my ashtray sits." — Bob Moore

'60s, he partnered with developer Kip Caudill and builder Braxton Dixon to turn a defunct petting zoo on the shore of Old Hickory Lake in Hendersonville into Caudill Estates. Among its earliest residents: Orbison and Johnny Cash, his famous wood-glass-stone home built by Dixon.

Moore's workload compelled him to stash several of his hand-carved basses at major studios around town to avoid needing to transport them. He reluctantly embraced electric bass, not using the one he owned until "Jim Reeves wanted it on something, and I had bought one from somebody and I think it was in self-defense. I never did like 'em. And so anyway, I had it in the car, and he said, 'Well, go get it and let's try it.' And so I did." He'd later use electric on Kenny Rogers' "The Gambler" and many other times, but he prefers upright acoustic.

A variety of producers drew on his talents, among them old friend Jerry Kennedy, an A-Team guitarist turned Smash Records producer. Moore was among the preferred group of A-Teamers Kennedy used behind Roger Miller (Moore's bass kicks off "King Of The Road"), Tom T. Hall, Faron Young and Jerry Lee Lewis. "When he'd set up a session…[Kennedy] would say 'Set the guys up'…to [his assistant] Trish, and Trish'd just call us all. We were his gang." At Epic Records, Billy Sherrill, known for tightly crafting his productions, used Moore often. He sensed the magic as Charlie Rich recorded his famous early ballad "Sittin' And Thinkin'." "I was sittin' right there. The setup in the Quonset hut…there was nothin' between me and [Rich's] left hand except the flat beside me where my ashtray sits. I'm sittin' just lookin' right down the keyboard, right beside him and it just run through me — that song."

It's hardly surprising that Bradley was his favorite producer. "Just put Owen at the top and that's where he'll always be," Moore says. In other cases, he recalls some sessions being more *lassiez-faire* than many realize. Historians

Hitmen, all (l. to r.): Kenny Lovelace, Jerry Lee Lewis, Bob Moore, James Burton, and Buddy Harman.

know Grady Martin was *de facto* producer of many '50s and '60s Columbia hits credited to Don Law, and that Ken Nelson, who gave his artists great latitude, heard every note and could step in. Atkins, Moore recalls, sometimes let session players or arranger Anita Kerr do the work. Hickory Records owner-producer Wesley Rose, Moore says, "would set in the control room and tell you, 'Go do what you want. I don't know nothin' about it!'"

Pappy Daily, who produced George Jones for four labels over fifteen years, had no real musical background. He, too, let the musicians do the heavy lifting, and he paid Moore extra to supervise Jones's 1965-71 Musicor recordings. With early session calls the next day, as 2 a.m.

approached, the bassist set limits for the often-inebriated star. "I said, 'I'm gonna give you this one more [take] and if you don't get it, I'm gone!' And 'course he didn't hardly get through the intro. I picked up and left. Pappy come runnin' out of the control room applauding, sayin' 'Thank God!'"

The late '60s brought a second wave of rockers, starting with Dylan. Moore came in to finish Moby Grape's 1969 *Truly Fine Citizen* album after bassist Bob Mosley quit during the Nashville sessions. That year, he and drummer Jerry Carrigan were the only Nashville players to back Chet Atkins on an album with Arthur Fiedler & the Boston Pops. He also worked on Dylan's *Self Portrait* sessions and with other rockers in addition to his country workload. The heavy schedule continued into the '70s, but it was inevitable that at some point an influx of younger artists, producers, musicians and new studios realigned the A-Team's makeup and lightened Moore's workload. He's philosophical about it today. "Several things added to this," he explains. "One of them being a natural phenomenon, and that's called attrition. Another part is my age. The younger producers have come in and brought their buddies, which always happens."

Moore, who divorced in 1975, abruptly retired in 1980 after the death of his fiancé. That self-imposed withdrawal lasted until 1981, when Crystal Gayle invited him to join her band for a yearlong world tour that rebooted his passion for playing. "The bad thing," he says, "is I had to play electric bass. I absolutely loved that part of my life and wish I could do it again." Not so a 1983 stint touring with Jerry Lee Lewis, which he recalls as "a disaster." Around that time, he met Kittra Bernstein, who'd worked in the Los Angeles music scene; they married in 1993.

Beyond performing, other opportunities came his way, including a chance to produce longtime friend Johnny Cash in 1989, after Cash's Mercury contract expired. Mercury then purchased eleven masters from Moore that became 1990's *Boom-Chicka-Boom*, considered by some Cash fans superior to his previous Mercury efforts or his final Columbia material. "He was still that guy from Arkansas," Moore reflects. "Cash's mystery is in his instant flow of simple words that make so much sense. I produced that album and he was the easiest guy to work with. It went just easy and pleasurable." Kittra suggested having Cash's mother Carrie

Nashville Cats (l. to r.): Hargus "Pig" Robbins, Ray Edenton, Bob Moore, and Harold Bradley.

secretly add her voice to the song "Family Bible," a surprise that moved Cash to tears when Moore first played it for him.

At their home in Franklin, Tennessee, Kittra catalogues her husband's musical legacy, using his session books and recordings. Moore himself is far from retired. He works on big-band recording projects, performs at Elvis festivals in Europe, tends to his properties in Florida, and does a few sessions. "I did a couple of Eddy Arnold things and a couple Ray Price things, and

James Taylor." — Bob Moore

Bob Moore (at right) sitting in with Jon Koonce at the Sutler Tavern in Nashville, 2004.

[for] some of my old buddies, people that I really liked from before," he says. "Nothin' on a regular scale — just on a one-by-one basis. They usually let me pick my band. I still like to work with all of them."

He still has a wish list. "I'd like to produce Anne Murray and James Taylor. They're two that I never got to work with that I always admired. Gordon Lightfoot — I always liked him and his songs. I like his writing and his delivery. I never got to work with him, either. There's probably some others, but that's the first ones that come to mind."

While his website includes a newer photo of him standing in front of his grandmother's old home on Long Avenue in East Nashville, the Nashville of Moore's youth is largely gone. So is the modest local music business centered around the Opry and WSM where his career began, superseded first by the vibrant, growing industry established by hits he helped create, and then — for better or worse — by 21st-century Music Row, with streets officially named "Music Circle" and "Music Square." Two facilities where he made history are historic sites: RCA Studio B and the Quonset Hut, part of the old Columbia Records complex now owned by Curb Records, who've been restoring the celebrated studio. Many of Moore's producer friends, artists he worked with, and A-Team cohorts are gone, most recently Buddy Harman, who died in 2008. He remains philosophical about it all.

"Nobody wants to be 76, but [considering] the alternative, then you do. I'm not enjoying knowin' that I have less years left than I did 25 years ago, but I have grown up enough to realize I need to enjoy and forget about the bullshit, and this is life and life is the same for everybody. And so, I'm enjoyin' what I do now. I enjoy that I've had the success that I've had. That don't mean I'm a Mickey Mantle and hit all the home runs in the world, but I've hit my share and so I'm happy about that. I'm happy that I got a lot of good friends, that I still have my health, and that I have enough wherewithal to get on through the rest of my life and then leave something to my kids and my wife. So I have to do my thinkin' every day."

As an ND *contributing editor, Rich Kienzle profiled pedal steel innovator Lloyd Green. He's interviewed thirteen other Nashville A-Teamers, among them Chet Atkins and Owen Bradley, for* Country Music *Magazine and their history publication* The Journal *(which he edited),* Guitar Player, Vintage Guitar, *and* Fretboard Journal, *as well as for Sony BMG Legacy and Bear Family Records.*

"...till the longest day is done"

IN PRAISE OF BOB MARTIN

by BILL FRISKICS-WARREN

Seeking out the poorer quarters, where the ragged people go
Looking for the places only they would know
— Simon and Garfunkel, "The Boxer"

Drunks, ex-cons, dispossessed souls and down-and-outers: These are Bob Martin's people, the scuffling anybodies who populate *Midwest Farm Disaster*, the Massachusetts native's recently re-issued 1972 debut, a record as unjustly marginalized as the lives it so compassionately inhabits. The populist spirits of Theodore Dreiser, John Steinbeck, James Agee, Walker Evans and Dorothea Lange suffuse the eleven songs on Martin's album. So do the discomfiting teachings of the Jesus of the gospels, who, as if to leave no doubt as to where God's sympathies lie, resolutely sought the company not of the rich

SHOCKO GRAFIX FROM A PHOTOGRAPH COURTESY BOB MARTIN

and powerful, but of prostitutes, lepers, and anyone else who might have been consigned to society's margins.

Modestly yet exquisitely wrought, Martin's record also calls to mind such justice-minded song-cycles as James Talley's *Got No Bread, No Milk, No Money…*, Si Kahn's *Home*, and Hazel Dickens' *Hard Hit Songs For Hard Hit People*. Echoes of roughly contemporaneous touchstones by John Prine, Bob Dylan, and Willis Alan Ramsey are evident as well. Yet these and other affinities notwithstanding, maybe the most singular thing about *Midwest Farm Disaster* is just how fully formed and prophetic it was — and still is, what with its allusions to recessions, foreclosures and third world wars.

"Blind Marie" is the song that I keep coming back to, the one track that, after having lived with Martin's record all fall, I still replay the moment it ends. The music's harmonic resemblance to several titles on *Blood On The Tracks* — a record that came *after* Martin's — is arresting enough. What lingers even longer with me, though, is Martin's ability, with a bracing lack of sentimentality, to reach across time and space and ennoble his protagonist, a blind street singer with whom he shares nothing in common other than a gift for singing and songcraft.

"All wrapped up/in her old brown coat/with her black face to the sun/Singing voodoo chimes/ and holy rhymes/till the longest day is done," he sings, cradling his fading memory of the woman and the sanctified blues she sang. "She burned up fast from the inside out/on that smooth Jamaica rum/Play that Jesus song for me/Blind Marie."

Solemnized with swells of piano and tender filigrees of acoustic guitar, Martin's tribute — as much a prayer as anything else — confers immortality upon a woman who was all but invisible to the revelers who shuffled in and out of the all-night diner near the street corner that once was her stage. "Blind Marie" conveys volumes not just about poverty and resiliency, but about the power of faith, art and memory, and in a mere three minutes and eight seconds.

Song after song on *Midwest Farm Disaster* distinguishes itself with an indelible opening passage. "I was born in the turning of the tide/in a mill town by the sea," Martin announces, in a keening rasp, at the outset of "Mill Town". From there he recalls how he and his parents and siblings never had anything on their table but their pride and yet how, all in all, those were good times.

"Changes In Me" begins with Martin confessing, "Had another bad dream last night/I wept most bitterly," while in the title track, his voice all but drained of emotion, he ominously reports: "Lorney Taylor died last week/She couldn't take no more." Two lines later, after telling us that the bank repossessed the Taylors' farm, he concludes that "Lorney Taylor died of grief/Just one farm in many that's been taken by a thief." Later, setting the scene in "Charlie Zink" — its protagonist a broke-down old-timer with wine dribbling down his chin — he observes: "Down behind the filling station/the old men talked in desperation/'bout what times had been/Everyone agreed they'd see better days."

Martin never strays from the poorer quarters, but from time to time he tempers the gloom with humor as wry as vintage Loudon Wainwright or John Prine. "Third War Rag" is kin to the latter's Vietnam-era send-up "Your Flag Decal Won't Get You Into Heaven Anymore." As the police shut down a free-for-all at the VFW, a donnybrook replete with strippers, belly dancers, and rivers of liquor, a guy at the bar glibly prescribes "another good war" as a pick-me-up for the stagnant economy.

In the riotous "Frog Dick, South Dakota," Martin waxes nostalgic about a town where just about the only thing its inhabitants have to croak about are the toilet seats they make at the town foundry. And yet even that product, he laments, has degenerated from wood to plastic. Wickedly deadpan, the song's opening stanza is worth quoting in full.

I wish I could go home again, to Frog Dick, South Dakota
For the annual sheep castration celebration the last week of July.
How fondly I remember, every ram we did dismember
How could I think to leave the town
That was the toilet seat center of the world?

Mordancy such as this raises the question of how an artist in command of wit as lacerating as Martin's — or, for that matter, empathy as profound — could slip through the chinks of pop history, especially at the height of the singer-songwriter era when "new Dylans" were being anointed each week.

An answer of sorts lies in the terse, three-paragraph section of Martin's bio unassumingly slugged "The Story." After an early fascination with the work of fellow Lowell, Massachusetts, native Jack Kerouac, Martin, we're told, went on to become a regular on the east coast folk circuit, where he was "discovered" at Gerde's Folk City, the New York club where Dylan rose to fame in the early '60s. A few years later, Martin was at RCA in Nashville recording *Midwest Farm Disaster* with the blessing of Chet Atkins. Not only that, he had the heady likes of David Briggs, Norbert Putnam, Kenny Buttrey and, the original LP's liner notes state, "various Nashville sidemen" in the studio supporting him.

By 1974, "The Story" goes on to explain, Martin had "dropped out of the mainstream and moved to a mountain home" in West Virginia, where he continued to write songs and eventually recorded his second album, *Last Chance Rider*, in 1982. Issued by folk-identified June

Bob Martin, then.

Appal Records (the audio component of the Appalshop filmmaking center in Whitesburg, Kentucky), the yet-to-be-reissued LP isn't the revelation that its predecessor is. Suffering in spots from a dated drum sound and synthesized strings, it nevertheless contains yet another batch of artfully plainspoken, if less than epic, originals.

Another decade would pass before the appearance of the self-released *The River Turns The Wheel*, a return to more topical — and, as heard in the title track, philosophical — songwriting. *River* also benefits from more sympathetic production, as well as from cameos by fellow New England folkies Bill Morrissey and Cormac McCarthy (not to be confused with the noted author of the same name). Martin's vocals and harmonica sound an even more Dylanesque note here, as they do on 1999's *Next To Nothin'*, an unvarnished gem that includes some of his most personal — and affecting — performances yet. The quietly urgent likes of "Ayla," "My Father Painted Houses," "Tryin'" and "Wrong Side Of Goodbye" are among the set's ruminative highlights. "Let Freedom Ring" is a rare but tonic anthem of protest.

It remains to be seen what Martin's forthcoming album of new material, produced by Jeb Loy Nichols and Jerry DeCicca, will bring when it arrives sometime in 2009. For now, however, *Midwest Farm Disaster* stands alone, not only because the record heralded the arrival of such a mature and visionary voice, but also for its relaxed, no-frills Nashville Sound. Technically speaking, you'd have to call the arrangements countrypolitan, particularly given the Muscle Shoals bona fides of Briggs and Putnam. As laconic and knowing as Martin's matter-of-fact delivery, the backing

of such soulful, empathetic musicians ensured that, as with such Nashville folk-rock classics as John Stewart's *California Bloodlines* and Dylan's *John Wesley Harding*, *Midwest Farm Disaster* would never sound dated. The record's crisp, un-cluttered production alone would make its reappearance an event; to discover such an original, prophetic voice at this late date, though, makes it a revelation. Even seemingly lighter fare such as "Old Rass," a paean to an old horse that could have been plucked whole from *A Confederacy Of Dunces*, contains such dire scenes as

Bob Martin today. Photographed by Phil Chaput.

"Grandpa sittin' in the Old Moose Cafe/Drinkin' liquor from a puddle on the floor."

Dispatches from the ranks of the Salvation Army and from the recesses of prison are here as well, but always with the driest of ironies and without a hint of condescension. "It's only been three days/since I left Deer Island Prison/but I can feel it start to be/the same old thing again," begins the closing track. The lines that follow might be easy enough to anticipate, but they still pack a wallop when, to a weary backbeat, Martin delivers them. "It's so hard to keep on the straight," he moans, "when your empty stomach makes your decision/And every wrong move I make/Bad luck has got my name."

Here again, a larger passage — in this case, the chorus, its commentary opening outward onto disinheritance that extends beyond any single individual — bears quoting in its entirety.

may seem, Martin nevertheless testifies to their possibility.

> *People on the street can you spare a dime*
> *Cast your bread upon my water.*
> *You've known the fat and easy times*
> *It all flowed back to you.*
> *How did the mill and the railroad kill*
> *The land we called our lady?*
> *Now she takes to the strip mine gang*
> *While her rivers run red to the sea.*
> *Thought I left Deer Island Prison*
> *But I can hear that whistle sound.*
> *Don't take too long in doing time*
> *To break a good man down.*

As sobering as such moments are, there remains something uplifting, or at the very least encouraging, about the humanity with which Martin seeks out these poorer quarters, as well as about the humanity, however broken, that he finds concealed within them. As remote as things like justice, or even just decency, may seem, Martin nevertheless testifies to their possibility. And not only to that, but to the prospect of some measure of redemption, even if all it involves is holding the memory of a blind street singer, a distraught farm woman, or an ex-inmate who remains a stranger to freedom in his aching consciousness.

ND *senior editor Bill Friskics-Warren is writing a book, under the working title* The Poorer Quarters, *about poverty and the human spirit.*

Live at McCabe's Guitar Shop, Santa Monica, California

a portfolio of photographs
by Roman Cho

I still remember seeing the photo of Jackson Browne, Elvis Costello, T Bone Burnett, Richard Thompson and Warren Zevon onstage together at McCabe's. T Bone is drenched in sweat, Zevon is bent at the waist pointing his guitar at the audience in a way only a rock star can, and all of them are smiling. Must've been a hell of a night. I was maybe 15, and lived a very long way from Santa Monica. A decade and a half later, living in Los Angeles in 2004, I was assigned to photograph Peter Case's show celebrating the 20th anniversary of his first solo gig at McCabe's. After the shoot, Lincoln Myerson, the concert director, extended an open invitation. Five years later, as you are reading these words, I will have concluded my tenure of documenting the McCabe's concert series, photographing Peter's 25th anniversary show. In those five years, I saw many young up-and-comers, mid-career artists and living legends grace the tiny stage, and witnessed many magical and transcendent musical moments to last my lifetime. Here are some photos from those five years. Enjoy. — **ROMAN CHO**

ONSTAGE: *Peter Case onstage (above left).* **WARM-ING UP:** *Tony Gilkyson (top); David Lindley (right); and Kasey Chambers and Shane Nicholson (above)*

BACKSTAGE: *(top) Dave Alvin and friends in the green room; (top right) John Hammond, centering himself; Freedy Johnston and Jackshit, re-hearsing (bottom right); Michelle Shocked (at right), walking toward the stage; and Mariee Sioux's hand-written set list (above).*

MEET THE PRESS: *Carolina Chocolate Drops (top); Marvin Etzioni (far right); Mary Gauthier (above right); the Creek Dippers (above left, l. to r.): Van Dyke Parks, Don Heffington, Victoria Williams, unknown.*

Dr. Ralph Stanley

Ramblin' Jack Elliott

ONSTAGE: *(top) Eight days before winning an Oscar, Swell Season's Marketa Irglova and Glen Hansard watch from the wings as Damien Rice plays an unannounced solo set (above); Loudon Wainwright III (far right); Cat Power (right); and Tom Russell (above).*

THANK YOU: *John Doe (above); Odetta (1930-2008) at right, in her final McCabe's performance.*

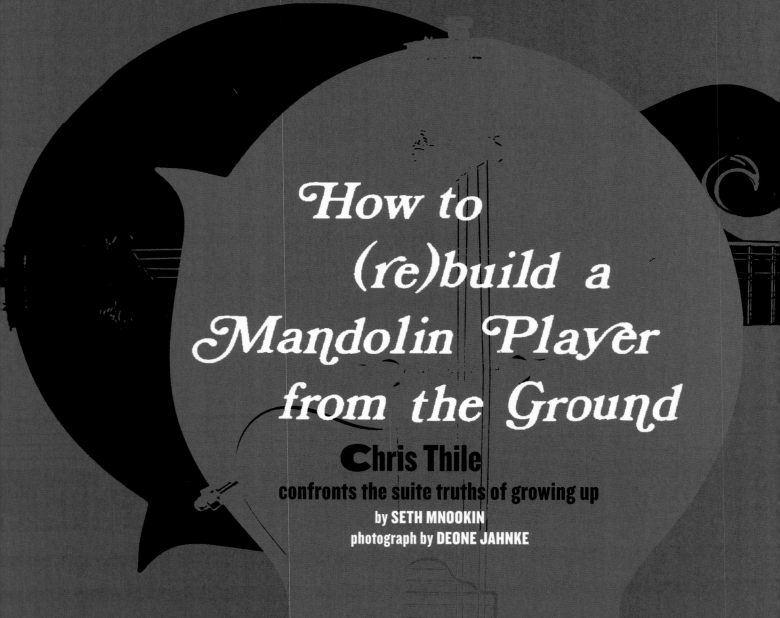

How to (re)build a Mandolin Player from the Ground

Chris Thile

confronts the suite truths of growing up

by SETH MNOOKIN

photograph by **DEONE JAHNKE**

I. Where the Skies are always blue.

TUESDAY, AUGUST 29, 2006 Chris Thile walks onstage and surveys the crowd. It's his first time headlining the Bowery Ballroom, the sine qua non of the Manhattan indie scene, and the room, which has an official capacity of 550, is almost full. A lot of unkempt sideburns and vintage eyeglasses are in the audience; a lot of tasteful tattoos peek out from under a lot of slightly-too-small T-shirts. Above the stage, in the two wrap-around balconies that bookend the upper level of this old vaudeville hall, are a dozen or so music writers and publicists, as well as label president Bob Hurwitz and a small knot of staffers from Nonesuch Records, the boutique Warner Music Group imprint. Nonesuch specializes in releasing albums by artists such as the Kronos Quartet, Brad Mehldau, and Wilco — serious-minded musicians whose work stretches across genres while straddling the line between avant-garde adventurousness and mass-market appeal.

The 25-year-old Thile (pronounced THEE-lee) loves being the center of attention, and after almost two decades of performing, he knows how to work a crowd. He's wearing what's been his de facto uniform as of late: jeans, sneakers, and an untucked button-down shirt and tie beneath a natty, rumpled blazer. Thile looks like he could be Jude Law's disheveled younger brother — there's the same golden-blond tussle of hair, the same aw-shucks acknowledgment of his genetic good fortune — but Thile's features are stronger, and he exudes an almost manic restlessness.

Once he settles in front of his microphone, he adjusts his shoulders, worries his knuckles, and bites a chunk out of the skin around the nail of his right index finger. Finally, he takes a breath and lowers his eyelids. The crowd falls silent as he lets a single note ring out from his custom-made Dudenbostel F5 mandolin. When the room is silent again, he picks another note, and then, with his eyes half-closed, he sighs out the line, "I am yours if you want me." A couple seconds later, as the vague discomfort that comes with witnessing this type of intimacy settles over the audience, Thile continues: "And I'm sorry if you do/Cause I don't have that much to offer..."

This show marks a pivot point in Thile's musical career, the moment at which the one-time prodigy begins to assert himself as arguably the most talented and influential person ever to play his instrument. Earlier in the day, Nickel Creek, the "progressive acoustic" phenomenon that Thile has starred in for the last sixteen years, announced that, after one final tour, it would go on an indefinite hiatus. Thile assembled the four other members of his new quintet — guitarist Chris Eldridge, bassist Greg Garrison, banjoist Noam Pikelny, and fiddler Gabe Witcher — because of his conviction that their ages, talents, and interests match up with his ambitions, which, at the moment, include finishing up work on a four-part suite he hopes will redefine the parameters and possibilities of the musical traditions in which he's been raised. (It's this project that Nonesuch has signed on to release.) Over the next two years, reviewers will christen Thile as the Bach of bluegrass and the Les Paul of the mandolin. If critical hosannas resulted in MacArthur fellowships, he'd have cashed that $500,000 check long ago.

At the moment, he's focused on the crowd at his feet. Nickel Creek regularly sold out

Bach of bluegrass and the Les Paul of the mandolin.

15,000-seat arenas, but now it's Thile's name atop the marquee, and he's playing in support of *How To Grow A Woman From The Ground*, an album that won't even be available in stores for another two weeks. By the time the show's first song ends, he's recognized a handful of faces from his recent drop-by gigs at the Living Room, an unassuming club about a half-mile east of here. Later, as Thile, Pikelny and I down cappuccinos at an East Village cafe across the street from Thile's apartment, he tells me how relieved he was that the audience was not made up of a bunch of people who'd happened upon a write-up in the listings section about a show by "the guy from Nickel Creek."

Pikelny, whose dry, needling asides offset Thile's never-ending patter, sees his opening. "That's funny," he deadpans. "I was paying attention to playing the music. You were just seeing who showed up." Pikelny looks at me. "He was multitasking. He's just that good."

INTERLUDE: BLUEGRASS, THE CLIFFS NOTES HISTORY (CHRIS THILE EDITION)

Bluegrass may be one of America's indigenous art forms, but like baseball and jazz, its origins lie on the other side of the Atlantic Ocean. The aching vocals and three-part harmonies that help define traditional bluegrass originated in folk idioms imported from the United Kingdom, most notably by Scottish immigrants who settled the Appalachians of West Virginia, Kentucky, and Tennessee. In the 1920s, the popularity of country acts such as the Carter Family married those high lonesome vocals to the fiddle music popular in the deep south. In 1944,

The Punch Brothers at the Station Inn, Nashville, Tennessee. Photograph by Autumn de Wilde.

five years after mandolinist and native Kentuckian Bill Monroe first settled on the appellation the Blue Grass Boys for his band, guitarist Lester Flatt and banjoist Earl Scruggs signed up with his band and supplied the dizzyingly fast runs that provided the genre's final ingredients. (Scruggs, who originated the three-finger picking style that allows for continuous runs of arpeggiated eighth-notes, was especially crucial in this regard.)

The music's fortunes have ebbed and flowed in the six decades since the end of World War II. In the early 1950s, Monroe and groups such as the Foggy Mountain Boys (the band that Flatt and Scruggs formed when they left Monroe in 1948) kept bluegrass at the forefront of American music through their perches at the Grand Ole Opry. After that came a period in which the country music establishment's rigid orthodoxy and the advent of rock 'n' roll made bluegrass seem more like an artifact than an active cultural presence. The folk revival of the late '50s sparked a romanticized appreciation of authentic "old-timey" music by young, hip music fans, and it was these new folk festivals that saved Monroe's career, keeping him from becoming a curiosity piece. By 1965, both Monroe and Bob Dylan were equally prominent draws at the six-year-old Newport Folk Festival in Rhode Island.

The success of Newport is part of what inspired Monroe to organize what's now recognized as the first national bluegrass festival, a multi-day affair in 1965 at a horse farm in Fincastle, Virginia. Ever since then, the festival circuit has played an integral role in the evolution and propagation of the music. In those early years, loose-knit jam sessions and parking-lot picking parties had a way of highlighting the ever-present tension in bluegrass between tradition and innovation. In 1967, after quitting his job as guitarist for Monroe's band, 25-year-old Peter Rowan teamed up with mandolinist David Grisman in Earth Opera, an outfit that was sufficiently experimental to open for the Doors. In the early 1970s, the Grateful Dead's Jerry Garcia put down his guitar and picked up a banjo for a series

New Grass Revival, 1986 (l. to r.): John Cowan, Bela Fleck, Pat Flynn, and Sam Bush. EMI promotional photograph.

of shows with Old And In The Way, a band in which Grisman and Rowan also played. When Sam Bush plugged in his mandolin in 1974, his band, New Grass Revival, gave this burgeoning movement a new name: newgrass.

The next true shift in the genre came in the 1980s, when cutting-edge musicians from the 1970s teamed up with younger aficionados as likely to be raised in the northeast as in the backwoods of Kentucky. In 1981, 23-year-old, New York-born, Juilliard-educated banjo prodigy Bela Fleck (named after Hungarian composer Bela Bartok) joined New Grass Revival. Over the next ten years, Bush, Fleck, Grisman, and a loosely connected group of musicians — including mandolinist Mike Marshall, dobroist Jerry Douglas, fiddlers Mark O'Connor and Stuart Duncan, bassist Edgar Meyer, and flatpicking guitarist Tony Rice — put out a series of breathtaking albums that borrowed heavily from the tradition of virtuosity and group improvisation in jazz. These collaborations reached their apotheosis with Strength In Numbers, a one-off supergroup starring Bush, Douglas, Fleck, Meyer, and O'Connor.[1]

After that surge of creativity, the 1990s were relatively fallow. Grisman's bands began incorporating flutes and mouth percussion to ill effect; the success of Fleck's electric combo, the Flecktones, led to a series of increasingly schlocky efforts; and when Rice's ill health forced him off the road, he focused on re-recording the classic bluegrass repertoire. The most notable new

[1] The band's sole release, *The Telluride Sessions* — named in honor of what is today one of the country's best-known bluegrass festival — features one track written by every possible combination of two musicians.

very much a part of, this tradition.

direction during these years was represented by the efforts of a handful of musicians — including Fleck, Meyer, and O'Connor — to marry bluegrass with chamber and classical music.

Thile is very conscious of, and has been very much a part of, this tradition. He grew up in Idyllwild, California, a small resort town in the San Jacinto Mountains that's halfway between Los Angeles and San Diego, and started playing mandolin when he was 5. At age 9, he formed Nickel Creek with 8-year-old fiddler Sara Watkins and her guitar-playing, 12-year-old brother Sean. Within a year, the trio, accompanied by Thile's bass-playing father, had become a popular attraction on California's regional festival circuit. Thile won a national mandolin competition when he was 12, at which point he was already writing sophisticated instrumentals. By the time he released his first solo record in 1994 at age 13, he was playing with bluegrass luminaries more than three times his age.

In 2000, the same year Alison Krauss's performance on the soundtrack to *O Brother, Where Art Thou?* helped spark a resurgence of interest in traditional American folk music, Krauss produced and championed Nickel Creek's eponymous debut on Sugar Hill, an independent label known for releasing records by everyone from Ricky Skaggs and the Seldom Scene to Doc Watson and Townes Van Zandt. The album, which eventually was certified platinum, resulted in an outpouring of critical acclaim for the band, including a group designation by *Time* magazine as one of five "Musical Innovators for the New Millennium." *This Side*, the band's second Sugar Hill recording, debuted at #18 on the *Billboard* charts in 2003 and later won a Grammy. By this point, it was readily apparent that Thile was not only the most talented member of Nickel Creek — his compositions were more melodically and rhythmically complex, his playing more engaging and adventuresome — but one of the most talented musicians the bluegrass world had ever seen. His 2001 solo release, *Not All Who Wander Are Lost*, might as well have been titled *Strength In Numbers: The Thile Sessions* — Douglas, Fleck, and Meyer are all featured, and the ease with which Thile used varied rhythms and meters on everything from Celtic instrumentals to multi-part compositions would have been astounding even if Thile wasn't still too young to drink.

II. Down the highway, down the tracks, down the road to ecstacy.

PART ONE: THURSDAY, SEPTEMBER 14, 2006 Thile is sitting outside and biting off chunks of skin from his fingers — a habit, he explains, that's the result of his inability to sit still. (There's also the fact that he needs to keep the nails on his left hand sufficiently trimmed to allow his distal phalanges — the last of the four bones that comprise the human finger — to make firm contact with the mandolin's fingerboard.) His hair is carefully tousled, his jacket well frayed, his red socks peaking out of bowling shoes. For the past hour, he's been riffing on Ricky Gervais, Elvis Costello and Cooperstown. (Thile — who, naturally, was the pitcher on his Little League team — is a Chicago Cubs fan and a baseball fanatic. His great-great-uncle is Big Sam Thompson, the

"You fall in love, you get married. For that not to work, and for me to come

19th-century Hall of Fame outfielder who held the single-season RBI record from 1887 until Babe Ruth broke it in 1921.)

He's also talking about the fundamental questions he's had to confront to get to where he is today. Growing up, Thile lived a remarkably sheltered and strait-laced life for someone so often in the public eye. When Nickel Creek's touring schedule caused him to miss too many classes, his parents decided to home-school him, a decision that made his family's fundamental brand of Christianity even more all encompassing. He fell in love with the first girl he ever seriously dated, and married her when he was barely 22. (A song on *Deceiver*, the 2004 solo record on which Thile plays every one of the 39 instruments, includes this cringe-inducing couplet: "I'm 19 and I've kissed two girls, that's all/You're 16, and you're one – is that against the law?") Even as his musical interests continued to expand — he sang lead on Nickel Creek's surprisingly credible cover of Pavement's "Spit On A Stranger" — his personal life stayed carefully conscribed.

Nickel Creek (l. to r.): Sara Watkins, Chris Thile, and Sean Watkins.

PHOTOGRAPH BY BRENT HEDGECOCK

All of that began to change when his marriage collapsed less than two years after it had begun and the edifice on which Thile had built his beliefs — that faith is always rewarded and good intentions are enough — began to crumble.

Soon, he realized his family's religious beliefs did not jibe with his view of the world. "I had to come to terms with things not being in black and white," he says. "I got divorced; it didn't mean I was a failure. I was raised really Christian, and ever since I was little kid, everything was always very polarized and clear and direct: You fall in love, you get married. For that not to work, and for me to come out of that not feeling like a miserable failure, was a challenge."

Thile's spiritual and physical liberation did not, as one might reasonably expect, result in his exploring another storied tradition in both country music and bluegrass: the conflict and anguish that results from the collision of deep-seated religious beliefs with the temptations of the flesh. (This tension is perhaps best embodied in Ira Louvin, whose struggles inspired the Louvin Brothers' 1960 record *Satan Is Real*, an album as well-known for its outrageous cover as for its songs.) From Bill Monroe to Hank Williams to Steve Earle, hard living (and loving) is one of the central narratives of bluegrass and country music.[2]

It's hard to imagine Thile being arrested for disturbing the peace; his acting-out consisted primarily of relocating from Los Angeles to New York, with some couch-surfing in Nashville thrown in along the way for good measure. If nothing else, he did begin, for the first time, to live a life that had a passing resemblance to those of his peers. He moved into an apartment in the East Village. He dated. He went to bars and hosted wine and cheese parties. But for the most

[2] Monroe engaged, as one biographer put it, in "compulsive skirt chasing." His decades-long affair with bassist Bessie Lee Mauldin produced both an illegitimate daughter and the inspiration for a number of Monroe's more plaintive numbers. It also resulted in a nasty wound when Monroe's wife Carolyn stabbed him in the leg with an ice pick.

out of that not feeling like a miserable failure, was a challenge." — Chris Thile

part, those were the limits of his indulgences. (Once, when I asked Thile if he'd ever smoked, he looked at me as if I were clinically insane.)

Thile's inner turmoil did result in as fertile a creative period as he'd ever experienced. The summer of his divorce, at a jam session in Nashville, he told Eldridge, Garrison, Pikelny and Witcher about a new composition he was working on — a symphonic suite that would entwine classical music with bluegrass and folk idioms while addressing the turmoil of his inner

life. "We said, 'Sounds great,'" Witcher remembered two years later. "'Can't wait to hear it.' I think we all assumed it would be with Stuart [Duncan] and Bela [Fleck] and those guys...and then he told us he wanted us to do it with him." When Thile showed the group some early notations he'd made, they thought it looked like "Chinese music." "I didn't think we could do it," Pikelny says. "He had more faith in us than we did."

At the time, all four were busy and successful musicians in their own rights: Eldridge was the guitarist in the Infamous Stringdusters, Garrison played regularly with jazz trumpeter Ron Miles, Pikelny was in Leftover Salmon, and Witcher had been playing professionally since he was 6. By the end of the year (2005), Thile had convinced them all to quit their other projects and work with him.

PART TWO: SATURDAY, MARCH 17, 2007 It's the second night of the John Adams-curated "In Your Ear, Redux" festival at Zankel Hall, the 600-seat auditorium located within Carnegie Hall. Adams, the American minimalist conductor and composer best known for his opera "Nixon In China," chose Nico Muhly, the classical music world's

Chris Thile, solo artist. Sugar Hill promotional photograph.

only bona fide trendster superstar, to open the three-day series. (Muhly's works have premiered at Lincoln Center and Tanglewood, and have been performed on the Tiber River in Rome and by the Royal Academy of Music. In one six-month period, he was profiled in *Smithsonian* and *The New Yorker*.) Tomorrow afternoon, Alarm Will Sound, a cutting-edge orchestra/band led by Alan Pierson, will conclude the three-day affair. (Pierson has conducted the London Sinfoni and the Silk Road Ensemble and collaborated with La Monte Young and Steve Reich.)

For tonight's program, Adams asked Thile and his band to premier *The Blind Leaving The Blind*, the name Thile settled on for the suite he had introduced to his bandmates nearly two years earlier. This, he told me recently, was his first effort at bridging the divide between formal music (where "every note is labored over") and folk music (which he defines as pretty much everything else). "What I've been trying to do is to consciously...share the development, have my mind share it with my heart, my mind share it with my instincts," he explained. This musical version of marrying nature and nurture can be tricky; if you're too rigid about combining the two, you end up favoring thought at the expense of instinct. "It's hard letting things happen and making things happen. That's what I want to do. That's my whole endgame."

If the audience doesn't pick up on the philosophical implications of Thile's work, they do appreciate the results. At the end of the show, as the band walks into the wings after the last of three standing ovations, Thile breathes in deeply and takes in the full scene one last time. Adams, sitting to the right of the stage, is beaming. As he gets slapped on the back, he keeps on repeating one phrase: "I know. I know."

III. A brand new pair of shoes.

PART ONE: FRIDAY, SEPTEMBER 28, 2007 Over the past year, the five musicians sitting inside the orchestra-sized recording room in Manhattan's Legacy Studios have been known as Chris Thile & How To Grow A Band, and Chris Thile & the Tensions Mountains Boys (which they decided sounded too much like their stage show would include hay bales). Finally, after dozens of dates around the country and hundreds of miles on their tour bus, the quintet settled simply on the Punch Brothers, a name they took from a Mark Twain short story. (In the story, the narrator is unable to stop humming a "jingling rhyme" that describes train conductors' daily duties: "Punch, brothers! Punch with care!/Punch in the presence of the passenjare!") They liked that handle for a couple of reasons: There's a rich history in country and bluegrass of "Brothers" bands going all the way back to Bill and Charlie Monroe, and the members of the group share a frustration with, as Thile puts it, "music that's being cranked out right now that's designed to be stuck in your head and take over your life in a way that makes you forget the difference between being familiar with something and enjoying something."

This is the second time in two years the Punch Brothers have booked studio time to record *The Blind Leaving The Blind*. The first time they tried to lay down tracks, they realized the piece wasn't ready for mass consumption — so they decided to make a straight-ahead bluegrass record instead. The result, 2006's *How To Grow A Woman From The Ground*, became "a way for us to find our footing together as a group," Thile says. It also was an opportunity for Thile to explore his musical roots. "The type of ensemble I've really felt comfortable writing for was always a bluegrass ensemble," he says. "That was my attempt to re-familiarize myself with those foundations — to make sure I understood where I was coming from."

To that end, *How To Grow A Woman* featured a rendition of Jimmie Rodgers' "Brakeman's Blues," one of Bill Monroe's early signature tunes, along with a handful of traditional instrumentals. The record's opener, "Watch 'At Breakdown," deliberately evokes "Whitewater," the opening track on Fleck's 1988 masterpiece *Drive*. "It's a blatant ripoff," Thile says. "I think ['Whitewater'] is one of the greatest opening tracks on any record, of any genre: there's Sam Bush popping, the banjo and the mandolin just fucking wailing in A." (Thile references key signatures as if they have the

to record this music is exhausting.

same significance for the average listener that they do to him.) "It is so fast and so powerful. I wanted to write something that had a similar introduction." Even the album's two pop covers — the White Stripes' "Dead Leaves And The Dirty Ground" and the Strokes "Heart In A Cage" — are translated in a way that's surprisingly effective and completely devoid of irony.

The Blind Leaving The Blind does not feature any similarly accessible entry points. Over the course of the piece's four movements, melodic themes twine around each other; tortuously beautiful sections sit alongside ones that blend chromatic and polymodal music. In one segment, counterpoint is employed by separating out 16th-note phrases into groups of four and groups of three and then having individual musicians move back and forth between the two, both during their own solos and while playing accompaniment.[3]

The concentration and commitment required to record this music is exhausting. Today's session didn't start until noon, but everyone arrived at least an hour earlier; Garrison later says he showed up at 10 a.m. to make sure he had enough time to warm up sufficiently. By 5 that afternoon, with a couple of hours still left at the studio, everyone is beat. The affection between the members of the group is immediately obvious. At any point in a conversation there's a chance any one of them could lapse into a pidgin that inserts 'r's after vowels, turning a word like "music" into "murusic." They use grade-school-esque nicknames: Eldridge is Critter, Pikelny is Pickles, and Thile is Hole, short for Speed Hole. (Thile

Chris Thile. Photograph by Shay Platz.

uses picks made by Michel Wegen, a model maker in the Netherlands. Wegen's bluegrass picks have seven small holes in them; Thile has jokingly said that he can alter his picking speed by covering and uncovering some of the openings.)

The disagreements they have are so minor as to seem nonexistent to outsiders. At one point during the session, Thile tells the group they're playing too aggressively, too frantically, and everyone needs to relax. Garrison says part of the problem is the canned solos; Pikelny says that's how he's going to have the most success; and Thile concludes with, "I wouldn't blame any particular problems on canned solos." During a break, Thile tells me I had just witnessed the band's "Behind The Music" scene. Johnny Rotten and Sid Vicious — or Mick and Keith, for that matter — it's not.

A couple of hours later, they call it a night. After watching the beginning of a Cubs game

[3] Rhythmic counterpoint, where, for instance, one part of a band is playing four-beat patterns and another is playing three-beat patterns, isn't all that common in popular music, but it isn't exceptionally rare, either. James Brown's "I Don't Want Nobody To Give Me Nothing (Open The Door And I'll Get It Myself)" is one example: the horn section and drummer are playing three-beat phrases while the rest of the band plays four-beat phrases. It's much less common to hear individual musicians moving back and forth between three-beat and four-beat phrases within a given section of a particular song.

on his laptop, Thile, the only member of the Punch Brothers who lives in New York, takes off to see his girlfriend, and the rest of us head up to 44X, a theater district restaurant known for its turkey and wild mushroom meatloaf and its buttermilk fried chicken and chive waffles. Over dinner, Eldridge, Garrison, Pikelny and Witcher joke about their self-appointed role as Thile's "advisory council" whose main function is affectionately to remind their friend how good he's had it.

Last year, the group opened for a band that's popular on the college circuit. Outside of the ten-grand payday, it was, everyone agreed, a brutal show: The audience wasn't paying attention, and the crowd's incessant chatter made it impossible for the band to hear themselves playing. Backstage, Thile looked crushed; he was, everyone agrees, truly miserable. Finally, one of them asked him if the show had been the worst musical experience of his life. Thile briefly mulled it over before deciding it was in the top two. "We've played weddings," Garrison laughs. "That show was nothing." The only other time the group says they've seen Thile look that uncomfortable was when they forced him to sit through a viewing of old Nickel Creek videos.

INTERLUDE: A BRIEF DISCOURSE ON "THE BLIND LEAVING THE BLIND" Ever since he began writing music, Thile has been upfront about the fact that his lyrics are directly drawn from the most intimate details of his personal life. (It's safe to say that Thile will never claim, as Dylan once did when asked about *Blood On The Tracks*, that his work is based not on his own experiences but on Chekhov's short stories.) Both with Nickel Creek and in his early solo works, this has resulted in a public chronicling of the awakening and maturation of a man whose sheltered upbringing fostered an almost touchingly naive precociousness.

The arc of *The Blind Leaving The Blind* both furthers and deepens this narrative through Thile's description of the immediate pain and lingering aftershocks of his divorce, an event that forced him to realize (albeit a bit later than most) that "the world doesn't always have your best interests at heart." The result is a bracing Bildungsroman that cycles through his ensuing struggles with powerlessness, impermanence, and acceptance. If the aspirations of Thile's earlier efforts didn't always match up with the subject matter, *The Blind Leaving The Blind* showcases a writer whose life has finally become suitable fodder for his ambition.

The process of learning to live with ambiguity is one of several themes that resurface throughout the piece. The intermittent lyrical sections that that are laced throughout the suite's 40 minutes are freckled with specifics — the fountain in San Diego's Balboa Park makes an appearance, as does a house (or is it a church?) at the top of San Francisco's Nob Hill — but these are used to convey a universal aching. As the piece goes on, Thile switches from first to third person and back again as he transitions from being defenseless and dependent to warily alone. He pleads with and denounces his lover, questions and rejects his God, leans on and embraces his friends. (The other members of the Punch Brothers even make an appearance in the work's penultimate stanza.)

Thile's true breakthrough, and the area in which he has the potential to be most transformative, is in the piece's arrangement and composition. The extent to which he uses each musician's

to be most transformative, is in the piece's arrangement and composition.

specific strengths is Ellingtonian in its specificity; it's hard to imagine *The Blind Leaving The Blind* without Eldridge's understated ability to float between open spaces and finger-knotting runs, Garrison's penchant for marrying bluegrass with jazz and modern music, Pikelny's ability to modulate the intensity and pitch of an instrument that often overwhelms everything around it, or Witcher's lush portamentos. (Thile even uses the limitations of his occasionally reedy voice as an advantage.) His acknowledged indebtedness to both Brahms' Fourth Symphony and Debussy's string quartet is readily apparent: There's the same cyclical revisiting of a central motif, the same skillful employment of key modulations, the same translation of key melodic phrases into idiomatic signposts. Thile's other influences and idols crop up repeatedly, but always in support of the overall intent. Listening to the suite never becomes an academic exercise, and you don't need to recognize how references to Bach butt up against ones to Radiohead and Robert Johnson to be overwhelmed by the piece's melancholic embraces, virtuosic interludes, delicate transitions, or flowing crescendos.

Thile's interest in composition would seem to fit in well with today's indie Zeitgeist, where a hint of classical shading can convey a lot of cool cachet. More than 35 years have passed since Frank Zappa went public with his Varese obsession. The rest of the 1970s saw a wave of out-there artists deliberately linking themselves to classical composers, ranging from Kraftwerk and its indebtedness to Stockhausen to the Grateful Dead's Phil Lesh and his oft-stated admiration for Charles Ives. Over the past decade, the avant-rock world has again nodded to classical traditions, albeit in a less theory-based and more superficial way: A handful of Canadian bands, including Arcade Fire, Broken Social Scene, and Godspeed You Black Emperor, have variously positioned themselves as working alternachestras; Joanna Newsom has mewled alongside the Sydney Symphony Orchestra and the Brooklyn Philharmonic; and Sufjan Stevens has looked to the Chinese Zodiac and the Brooklyn-Queens Expressway as inspiration for his precious symphonic efforts.

Those touchstones might help translate Thile's music to the college radio station aficionados who packed the Bowery Ballroom, but his work can be better understood when seen in the context of efforts by a small band of acoustic artists who have been doing their part to blur the boundaries between what Thile would refer to as formal and folk music. Bela Fleck and Edgar Meyer have been particularly active in this regard, and their Sony Classical collaborations are stunning efforts to redefine and re-imagine disparate musical languages. Coming from the other direction is cellist Yo Yo Ma, whose translations of Argentinean tango master Astor Piazzolla and collaboration with Italian film composer Ennio Morricone are almost as well-known as his renditions of Brahms' Sonatas for Cello and Piano.

A less obvious point of reference is Brad Mehldau, Thile's Nonesuch labelmate. Mehldau is often compared to Bill Evans, another white jazz pianist known for both his trio recordings and his history as a heroin addict, but that easy encapsulation obscures Mehldau's abilities. Mehldau's penchant for interweaving right-hand motifs while simultaneously toying with time and key signatures is similar to Thile's exploration of ostinatos in his own recent work. Both have the ability to translate modern-day pop songs in a way that doesn't sound the least bit contrived. (In fact, both are particularly adept at repurposing Radiohead songs: Mehldau's version of "Paranoid Android" is revelatory, as is the Punch Brothers' take on "Morning Bell," which, for the moment at least, is officially unavailable.) Not surprisingly, Thile is a huge fan of Mehldau. "You can hear the admiration with which he approaches [pop songs]," Thile says. "It's not genre busting. It's not gimmicky. It's awareness that it's really all the same shit and that you can learn from everything, and that you *should* learn from everything, and it's your duty as a responsible musician to learn from everything and to be able to appreciate the good in all kinds of music."

IV. Everyone is So near.

PART ONE: SUNDAY, FEBRUARY 10, 2008 In three days, the Punch Brothers will depart on a 15-date run that'll bring them from Paducah, Kentucky, to Tacoma, Washington. Plenty of logistics are still to be worked out, including which mandolin Thile will bring on the road — he's on the verge of retiring his Dudenbostel for a 1924 Lloyd Loar Gibson F-5, the same type of mandolin Bill Monroe used throughout his career.[4] Thile's new instrument produces a more muscular sound, compared to what he's jokingly called his "sissy boy" setup. The Gibson, Thile says, is a "cannon," and as he sits with Pikelny at that same cafe across from his apartment, he wonders if he has enough time to break it in. "C'mon," Pikelny says. "You gotta bring the Loar."

Just because Thile is using the bluegrass equivalent of Louis Armstrong's trademark trumpet does not mean he has any particular reverence for the mandolin or its masters; quite the contrary, in fact. "Listening to mandolin players has not been a big part of my development," he says matter-of-factly when asked for his opinion of one of the more popular players of the last 40 years. Perhaps not coincidentally, his style is in stark contrast to Monroe's: Thile's playing is marked by exquisitely deliberate runs that extend far up the fingerboard, while Monroe remains the leading example of a mandolinist whose metronomic chopping takes full advantage of the instrument's percussive qualities. "The instrument is so young," Thile says. "In terms of technique, it's such a work in progress….Every mandolin player, including myself, falls way short, as far as what the music should be, and so ultimately it just smacks of failure to me when I hear it. Every time I hear it, there's this sound in my head that we can't approach yet." Over the next several decades, Thile predicts a period of rapid evolution "until finally there's a culmination of technical achievement — like a Segovia on the guitar, someone like Chopin or Gould on the piano, a Heifetz or a Paganini on the violin. I don't think my instrument has seen anybody like that."

This degree of deliberate reflection is rare in popular music. Within bluegrass circles, Thile has a reputation for being overly intense, and more than once, fellow musicians have chided him (and more recently, the other four Punch Brothers) for not enjoying music as much as he should. "I almost never go to live shows," he says. "If I'm sitting there listening to music and it's not good, I feel like I'm wasting my evening." This isn't conveyed arrogantly; it's simply a statement of fact. "I could be at home listening to Bartok, or practicing. Also, I rarely find anything that's new. And that's what I want to hear."

[4] Loar, a famous luthier during the '20s and '30s, introduced a longer neck, a floating fingerboard, and two F-shaped holes on either side of the instrument. His Gibson F-5's are the Stradivariuses of the mandolin world, and they generally go for somewhere between $200,000 and $250,000.

as far as what the music should be..." — *Chris Thile*

Punch, the album that's the end result of the songs Pikelny, Thile, and the rest of the band first began working on almost three years earlier, hits stores in two weeks. (In addition to *The Blind Leaving The Blind*, there are four other tracks on the album, all of which are credited to the band as a whole.) "I put it on for probably the first time in more than a month yesterday," Thile says. "I had to take a break. It's hard to listen to." That, of course, is Pikelny's cue: "Because of your mistakes on the mandolin parts? Because, you know, I'm fine with how I played on the record." Thile laughs, but doesn't break his train of thought. "I just heard it so many times, I lost perspective. But I'm really pleased with the arc, the big-picture stuff. I actually feel great about that. I feel like it tells a story, both the lyrics and the music. I like how the parts fit together — the prologue, the epilogue, the themes. I feel good about that. I think it rings true."

The new Punch Brothers (l. to r.): Noam Pikelny, Chris Eldridge, Paul Kowert, Chris Thile, and Gabe Witcher. Photograph by Cassandra Jenkins.

Thile's satisfaction with the construction of the piece represents more than just the successful completion of his latest musical project. In one of our first conversations, Thile told me, "The only thing that's ever been really comfortable to me is playing." He tries to practice for between three-and-a-half and five hours a day — any less, and he doesn't feel like he's improving; any more and he risks hurting his wrists. Despite this devotion, Thile says he's begun to derive more artistic satisfaction from composing than from playing. "I hope I'm not ill-suited to that," he says. "I just get far more pleasure from writing music than I do out of acquiring facility on [the mandolin]."

PART TWO: WEDNESDAY, FEBRUARY 20, 2008 Eleven months after they appeared at Carnegie's Zankel Hall, the Punch Brothers are at Jazz at Lincoln Center's Allen Room, another New York performance space that wraps the tradition and prestige of a puffed-up cultural institution in modern packaging. The Allen Room opened five years ago in Manhattan's version of a Middle America strip mall park: the Time-Warner Center, a structure whose two monoliths tower 750 feet above Columbus Circle. The wall behind the Allen Room's stage is made entirely of glass, giving the audience a glimmering nighttime slideshow of taxicabs snaking around Central Park. As Thile steps up to his mike, he looks over his shoulder and references the spoken-word interlude in Stevie Wonder's "Livin' In The City": "New York," Thile says. "Just like I pictured it."

During performances, Thile can be, in turns, cheeky, self-effacing, and mildly cocky. He tells the crowd that if the band sucks, it won't matter — at least the view is great. After fumbling through an introduction, he stage-whispers, "I sound so stupid." Between his suite's first and second movements, he admits that he considered asking the audience to hold their applause until the end of the piece, "but then we were worried you wouldn't applaud at all." And when it looks like that night's lunar eclipse won't occur until after the show is done, he says, "It's His fault. He's known about it for weeks." (Thile's next quip — "Ooooh, Nickel Creek humor" — went over the heads of everyone in the audience whose familiarity with Thile didn't extend to an awareness of the overt religiosity present in some of his previous band's work.)

The fans (and the critics) in the audience lap it up. Both *The Blind Leaving The Blind* and "Morning Bell" are received with deservedly rapturous applause. A review in *The New York Times* compares Thile to "a great classical guitarist" who can toss off "witty, jazz-flavored bluegrass solos with breathtaking velocity," adding that "his technique is merely the starting point" for an artist who is expanding the frontier of "American country-classical" music.

On Friday morning, the band will fly across the country for six dates on the west coast. Thile will have his Loar with him, and months' worth of concerts have been planned out. Later in the year, he'll be recording an album with Edgar Meyer, whose classical work has been "an inspiration." "There's a lot going on," he says. "It'll be a busy year. That's good. That's very good."

Epilogue: *I'm just saying.*

By the end of 2008, the Punch Brothers' place in the acoustic music world had become more defined. For all their success, the band never quite reached the level of a bona fide crossover phenomenon, and while the vast majority of mainstream critics greeted the band with ecstatic acclaim, the hard-core bluegrass world hadn't been as universally receptive.

Audiences' reactions seemed equally mixed. While shows in the country's urban centers — New York, San Francisco, Seattle and the like — attracted fervent crowds several thousand strong, many smaller markers weren't as immediately receptive. It seemed as if there would always be fans who wouldn't be happy unless Thile was picking along to "My Old Kentucky Home." (During a show at a folk festival in Scotland, a fan shouted, "Play some fucking bluegrass!" in the middle of a particularly quiet section of *The Blind Leaving The Blind*.)

The band's identity also became more settled. While Eldridge, Pikelny and Witcher all moved to New York, Greg Garrison, the oldest member of the original quintet, decided to stay in

Edgar Meyer (left) and Chris Thile at the Ryman Auditorium during AMA conference, Nashville, Tennessee, September 2008. Photograph by Deone Jahnke.

Colorado with his family. In November, Paul Kowert, a 22-year-old who had toured with Mike Marshall, replaced Garrison. Thile, meanwhile, spent a good chunk of the fall touring with Meyer in support of the two artists' stunning collaboration, an eponymous effort that was released by Nonesuch in October.

In the course of all our conversations, Meyer is the only musician I heard Thile speak of with a sense of reverential awe. Meyer — who, in addition to being the first bassist to win the Avery Fisher Prize for outstanding achievement in classical music, actually did win a MacArthur genius fellowship — is equally effusive. "There is no one who is more remarkable and talented than Chris," Meyer said shortly after the duo's fall tour had concluded. "Part of what separates him is that you can't put a finger on what separates him....He's never displaying the full range of what he can do at any one moment. There's always more, and he's striving to get the big picture and not just show off one or two abilities. I haven't seen a package like that – well, I haven't worked with the great jazz pianists, but there's nobody like that in my circle."

Separate from what he accomplishes commercially, Thile has more to achieve before he can lay claim to be truly transformational. His artistic voice is not yet fully developed — unlike John Coltrane or Bob Dylan, Thile has not developed a musical language that's immediately identifiable as being his own — but both *The Blind Leaving The Blind* and his work with Meyer show he's well on his way. If he ever gets there, he'll have helped uncover a new path to the future.

Seth Mnookin lives in Brooklyn with his wife and their cat. He began his professional career writing about music for Addicted To Noise, *a defunct online music magazine, and is presently a contributing editor at* Vanity Fair, *where he covers politics, media, and national affairs. He's the author of two books:* Hard News *(Random House, 2004), about the recent history of* The New York Times, *and the national bestseller* Feeding The Monster *(Simon & Schuster, 2006), about the year he spent living with the Boston Red Sox. For more information, visit www.sethmnookin.com.*

RECKLESS EMOTION

A CONVERSATION WITH CHRIS HILLMAN ABOUT THE FLYING BURRITO BROTHERS

by BARRY MAZOR

photograph by ROMAN CHO

(and mistreated by SHOCKO GRAFIX)

"Gram Parsons had the charm, the charisma — and the voice.

The list of Rock and Roll Hall of Fame inductees who have also charted records in the country top ten is short and select, and almost everyone on it comes from the rockabilly era — Elvis, the Everlys, Jerry Lee Lewis, Carl Perkins, Gene Vincent, Brenda Lee. Chris Hillman is a pivotal, even instrumental performer of a later vintage. Inducted into the Rock Hall for his key role with the Byrds in the 1960s, Hillman also had two #1 country singles (and seven top-tens) with the accomplished Desert Rose Band in the late '80s. Along the way, he's been in other well-known rock outfits (Manassas, Souther-Hillman-Furay) and bluegrass bands (from his earliest performing days with the Scottsville Squirrel Barkers and the Hillmen). And, here in the 21st century, he still packs houses with his cross-genre solo shows or in duo outings with Herb Pedersen.

But for all the times he has talked about his 45 years as a songwriter, musician and singer, what so many have wanted to know more about most is the period of less than three years when he was out front with the groundbreaking country-and-rock-concatenating Flying Burrito Brothers – at first, of course, with co-leader and songwriting collaborator Gram Parsons. He'd spoken of that experience only sparingly until the recent publication of *Hot Burritos: The True Story Of The Flying Burrito Brothers* (Jawbone Press), a collaboration between Hillman and author John Einarson. Einarson, a Canadian, had previously written *For What It's Worth: The Story Of Buffalo Springfield* and the turn-of-the-'70s scene and era portrait *Desperados: The Roots Of Country Rock*, as well as, most reassuringly for Hillman himself, *Mr. Tambourine Man: The Life And Legacy Of The Byrds' Gene Clark*.

In *Hot Burritos*, Hillman addresses the story of that fabled outfit with the fabled outfits in detail, pulling no punches. The unraveling of what was initially his close working and personal relationship with the near-legendary Parsons is inevitably a key focus. He depicts the Burritos' original, most regularly celebrated lineup as one with grand ambitions and often feeble execution. But for all of that, Einarson suggests the Flying Burrito Brothers should be in the Country Hall of Fame, which would seem an unlikely outcome, practically speaking, beyond the mention of Gram on the new plaque marking Emmylou Harris's induction.

Hillman himself agrees in print that for all of the missed opportunities, there was also magic afoot. That leaves some questions of interest, and I recently had a lengthy talk with Hillman so that *No Depression* could ask them.

NO DEPRESSION: How did the book, with the focus specifically on the Burrito Brothers part of your life and music, come to be? And why now, and not before?
CHRIS HILLMAN: Be it known, Barry — I loved the Flying Burrito Brothers, but that was a very small part of my musical career. And you've got to remember, I was coming off of the Byrds, a band musically proficient enough to have gone from doing Bob Dylan's songs to cutting "Eight

I was there to help him...." — Chris Hillman

Miles High" within about the same two years' time I was with the Burrito Brothers. Going from *that,* to playing this really sloppy country music; that's how I see it now.

Gram Parsons had the charm, the charisma — and the voice. I was there to help him, to make that happen, and to keep things in order....So the book conjures up some bad memories for me — not just the events, but that *I* allowed them to happen. In all honesty, I was reluctant even to bother with it at first — but I *like* John Einarson. He did an incredibly good job with his Gene Clark biography; his research in his books is accurate, he's factual, and he's very unbiased as he approaches his subject.

ND: The book jacket copy talks about "shattering myths," and there is, it seems, something of a debunking approach in a lot of the telling.

CH: I don't see it as debunking a myth as much as showing how we got from point A to point B. I loved Gram dearly. He was an unbelievably gifted, talented man who had the wherewithal to do anything he wanted to, and some of *those* things knocked him off of the starting team. He made those choices — and it reached a point where I couldn't work with him, as you know. It just was so uncomfortable.

These are all things that happened 35 years ago, and, yes, there was a time when I would see someone talking about "Gram Parsons' beautiful composition 'Sin City'" and I'd go "Hey; I had half that song

The Byrds, ca. 1967 (l. to r.): Chris Hillman, David Crosby, Michael Clarke, and Roger McGuinn. Photograph by Don Hunstein.

written before he was awake!" And my wife would look over and say, "Honey, would you like to trade places with him right now?" Ouch!

But the fact is, I wrote some of my best songs with Gram, and I hope this book helps set the record straight. Some of the very best material I've ever co-written with somebody was with him, for that first album. There were some gems on there that we felt, felt in our hearts. It was a very, very productive, creative time, and we were very close then, sharing a house and working. It was a great time.

ND: In some ways, nobody knows any better than you what he was "really like..."

CH: He was an interesting guy; there's no doubt about that. His whole background was so Tennessee

Williamsesque! Lots of money and insanity and alcoholism, that whole negative stigma of new money in the old south. And it's what led to his early demise. Here was this kid — extremely bright, intellectually — who had a $50,000-a-year trust fund. That was partially to blame for his destroying himself — and for strained feelings. The rest of us were all starving, living from hand to mouth, and he didn't have to do that. His stepfather and mother *bought* him a nightclub to perform in when he was 16!

That kind of stuff is pretty harmful in the long run. I have great empathy for Gram growing up; my God in heaven, what he had to go through. We'd shared that both of our fathers had died. And I *knew* those people; the stepfather, Bob Parsons — he was the sort of guy where you'd count your fingers after shaking his hand. It was like a bad movie. There's nothing more in life I wanted than to see him succeed — because Gram had the goods. I didn't have them yet then; I was in my apprenticeship stage — but he had the goods.

ND: How screwed up *is* the record, as you see it — whether it's due to all those Gram Parsons books (at least six), blind speculation, romanticizing — or anything else?

CH: I want people to know that I think we had a great *vision* — and that I was to blame as much as Gram that we didn't fulfill it as professionally and diligently as we could, taking that vision and turning it into a real musical statement, on record or onstage.

The Flying Burrito Brothers, live in 1969 (l. to r.): Gram Parsons, Michael Clarke, Chris Hillman, Chris Ethridge, and Sneaky Pete Kleinow. Photograph by Craig Folkes.

Live onstage we were really awful. One of the worst records I've ever had my name on, in 45 years, was *Live At The Avalon Ballroom 1969,* which came out about a year ago, on Amoeba. I weakened on that, because certain people needed the money that was offered as an advance; Pete Kleinow had died and his daughter Anita had been stuck with huge medical bills, and Chris Ethridge was flat broke. That, like the bootlegged versions put out for years, got to me. I'd been playing on "Eight Miles High" and now look at *this*! When I was 18 years old and playing in the Scottsville Squirrel Barkers, that band could have blown that off the stage!

ND: But you wouldn't say, I take it, that with the Burritos, well…'nothing was delivered.'

R&B songs and then redoing them country." — Chris Hillman

CH: People should understand that with the Burritos we really were treading on undiscovered ground. Where Gram really shone, where he was brilliant, was taking these R&B songs and then redoing them country. Not that this connection hadn't been made by Ray Charles already, but there was a different angle when Gram took up a song like "Dark End Of The Street." And it was certainly breaking new ground to cut a song like "Do Right Woman" from Aretha Franklin from a man's point of view!

ND: I'd say that those were among his best vocals on record.

CH: Absolutely right. And the best vocals he did on records, ever, were on that first album, too — on "Hot Burrito 1 And 2." Very heartfelt, very soulful. That's what was trying to get out; he had the emotional depth, and the interpretation, but *that's* the point where he could also get it out there, doing it professionally. I didn't have that emotional depth as a singer yet; it wouldn't come from me for a few more years. I wish I'd had more confidence back then, but it didn't happen that way.

ND: Through much of *Hot Burritos*, you and John spell out just how messy the original Burritos lineup's music could be, live and in the studio, and the opportunities missed. But for all that, near the end, you also say that the '68-'69 band with Gram — the one that made *Gilded Palace Of Sin* — "had the magic." There's a succession of songs on that first LP that can still stun. I've seen the strong reaction in your solo shows when you sing "Wheels," for instance. When the songwriting collaboration with Gram Parsons was working — how did it work? And when it wasn't, what had happened?

CH: When it worked it was really back and forth — lyrically and melodically. We were on the same page; it was almost second-guessing the next line with him and vice-versa. The true story of "Sin City," and I'm not patting myself on the back with this, is that I did come up with that first verse, and part of the chorus, and I woke him up. I said "I really think there's something interesting here: 'This old town is filled with sin; it will swallow you in...'" Well, I'd just gone through a divorce, and all of this garbage, and that song really wrote itself.

But he came up with the "green mohair suits" stuff, a fascinating line, and then it went off on some abstract thing about being at Whisky a Go Go on Sunset Strip. It was a microcosm of the culture at that particular time. This song was sort of our little chronicle of the time — but it's relevant right now. And Robert Kennedy, by the way, was the man who "'came around, tried to clean up this town."

"Juanita" was a true story about this girl that I met, and "Wheels," well, Gram had crashed his motorcycle. Everything had something that spurred it. "My Uncle" — Gram gets his draft notice in the mailbox while we're living in the San Fernando Valley, and we ran in and wrote that one in twenty minutes. I know that Steve Earle's cut it, to bring that sort of Vietnam-era draft-dodger theme into current events, which actually works quite well.

ND: How did you first know that this special sort of collaboration was going to be possible?

CH: The day Gram auditioned for the job in the Byrds, he started doing "Under Your Spell Again." I went, "Whoa! This guy knows who Buck Owens is!" Nobody in the Byrds knew that — except me, coming out of country music, and I immediately hit the harmony part with him. That was the first moment; it was about something we both connected on.

"Talk about 'alternative country' music; that's what we were.

Gram knew his country music. You've gotta remember something: Emmylou Harris, when I first heard her playing in Georgetown, was not singing country music; she was singing folk, like Carolyn Hester, Joni Mitchell or Joan Baez. Gram gave her a hell of a musical education, a quick course in the 30 or 40 percent of country that's good music! I mean, I might have worked with Emmy then, but I didn't see where she could fit into the Burrito Brothers at the time. So in writing these songs, we had that point of origin that both of us were steeped in.

Sweetheart Of The Rodeo with the Byrds wasn't my favorite album, but it was a noble experiment. And Gram was the guy who brought stuff to that party — "One Hundred Years From Now" and "Hickory Wind," two of his greatest tunes, and he sang them. Even with the mixup over legalities of using his vocals, Gram sang those pretty darned good. He always had a bit of a pitch problem, but when he was there emotionally, that overrode any technicalities. He was on the money with those two songs. Roger [McGuinn] and I weren't writing anything at the time; we were like old, grizzled veterans who'd been hammered and kicked around over four years, and here we were, now, holding the band together.

ND: Whatever the limitations were, how do you see the Burritos' lasting musical contribution — the real reasons for still talking about that short-lived band?

CH: Nobody is aware of creating some sort of legacy at the time. You're doing it, and it's trial by error; you're sort of doing something you feel. It's all heart-driven. It wasn't a big leap for us to do a country album. With what we did with *Sweethearts*, and then going right to *The Gilded Palace Of Sin*, the door was opened for people who were normally rock music FM radio listeners to find this interesting, and then go on to discover more of it. I think those two albums did usher in a greater appreciation of country music — and that was despite all of the country-rock that came out of California, some of which I thought was fluffy.

But the Burritos were, I thought, the ultimate outlaw soul band. Talk about "alternative country" music; that's what we were. We started that. If there's any claim to fame, it's that we started the alternative movement that you still hear today. There was nobody doing that.

ND: I was a college DJ in Washington, D.C., in those years, and I'd play those records, and it's certainly true that not everybody who listened to rock or listened to country got what it was all about. And they'd not always be shy about calling in and saying so!

CH: There was the funny story with Ralph Emery, the DJ in Nashville, where he had *The Gilded Palace Of Sin* tacked on the wall outside of his office, and with a big red pen it said, "This is *not country music.*" Roger and Gram had gone to do an interview with him when we were all still with the Byrds, and Ralph was such a jerk to them then that they wrote that song "Drug Store Truck Driving Man," a classic! I wish I'd written a part of that. But later, whenever I'd go on his show with the Desert Rose Band, Ralph would ask, "Did *you* write that song?" Finally, I had to say, "No, but I wish I had!" So when Roger was on later, Ralph would say, "Well, how is Gram doing?" and Roger would answer, "He's still dead." McGuinn was pretty darned quick in those situations!

ND: What separates the Flying Burrito Brothers from many later bands who reference them is that the country songs you covered live were not just some retro, old country revival deal, but very often pretty new songs from Buck Owens, Merle Haggard, George Jones, Conway Twitty.

We started that." — Chris Hillman

Fresh, current choices of the day, like, say, Conway's "The Image Of Me," that rockers were unlikely to know. The tendency now is for bands not to do current country songs but, oh, "Six Days On The Road," the same old ones that worked then.

CH: Well, *we* did "Six Days On The Road" because Taj Mahal did a really good version of it with Jesse Davis on guitar and Chuck Blackwell on drums, and we'd done shows wth Taj all over L.A.! But you're absolutely right; we would also cover songs that were hits on the radio, but obscure to people, like Johnny Bush's "Undo The Right," a song Willie Nelson had written.

ND: How were those country song choices made? Were they the stuff on your own record players, or how did you guys come to them?

CH: We were so into it. I mean Gram and I, in our closest time together, when we were putting the band together, there were many times when we'd drive out on a weekend to the Aces Club, in the City of Industry, which is an industrial suburb south of L.A. People would be playing country music 24 hours a day. JayDee Maness would be up for hours there playing steel; that's how long I've known JayDee. We'd get up there at four in the morning, on Friday, and we'd start singing "Under Your Spell Again"

The Desert Rose Band, 1988 (l. to r.): Steve Duncan, Herb Pedersen, Bill Bryson, Chris Hillman, JayDee Maness, and John Jorgenson. Photograph by Peter Figen.

or "Above And Beyond" or something, all kinds of stuff, and just go for it. It was pretty interesting. That's called passion for music — no "Gee, how much money are we gonna make?" That never entered our minds, to the point that it eventually did affect the band, because we did have to live.

ND: What was the country response to your material like?

CH: Even when we played the Palomino, the old country club, I can remember one night, Chris Ethridge was still playing with us, and we were up there, just trying to get through it, and Sneaky [Pete Kleinow], too. Some old guy was in the bar and he turned around and yelled up at Chris, "Get back on the cross!" Meaning, he wasn't so knocked out by this; they liked it, but they were used to really good bands coming there, and we really weren't up to that level. Some of those bands were just letter-perfect, because they had to be; it's how they made a living. We were just sort of *laissez-faire*, coming into it with that hippie outlook.

"...though the early '60s were very creative and idealistic, the whole behavior

The Burrito Brothers always drew a most diverse crowd, including some of the Rolling Stones, or Marlon Brando, when we'd work at the Corral out in Topanga Canyon, or at the Palomino. Those were good times — until it got to the point when we were still working those clubs, and Gram would show up late.

In the book, we retell that now-famous story of me having to go to the Stones' sessions to get him, and finding Mick actually chewing him out. Mick Jagger's a very professional guy. People forget that all of the English bands, the guys my age, grew up in post-World War II Britain, very poor. The country had been hammered, and they had nothing. The monarchy had some money, but everybody was pretty much flat on their back. So those guys have a different mindset about getting the opportunity to make money doing something they love to do. Mick was not that fond of Gram toward the end, because he was looking at this kid who didn't put any time into his craft, and he was affecting Keith and ultimately, *their* band's purpose.

Chris Hillman and Herb Pedersen.

ND: At times, it seems that at least some latter-day rockers who celebrate and reference the Burritos see you as a gang that sang heartbreak songs and married that to the loosey-goosey, even self-destructive aspect that you were not entirely in love with. They celebrate the Burritos precisely *because* the band, particularly Gram, was an accident waiting to happen!

CH: Exactly, the whole myth of that. So many of those who died young become icons, in a sense, and it's pretty hard to beat Gram's death for details, with the burning coffin and all that — but it's almost *creepy.*

I look back on the '60s a little differently now. I'm older, a little more conservative, and looking back, I had a great time; don't get me wrong. I got to do something that one percent of the population gets to do, and I got paid very well for doing something I loved to do. I'd taken a lot for granted and didn't maybe really appreciate that enough until the last twenty years, but my point is that though the early '60s were very creative and idealistic, the whole behavior of our generation got to be like kids in a candy store, running around, tearing down some rock-solid traditions that had kept civilization alive and growing for centuries.

I mean, OK, that's a broad statement, but when people look back on all of that with rever-

of our generation got to be like kids in a candy store...” — Chris Hillman

ence, saying, “Wow; that must have been cool!” I just look back and go, “I could have done my job better.” It *did* look like an accident waiting to happen! Being loaded on the stage? That’s just embarrassing.

ND: I take it that after that first, celebrated Burritos LP, things went south pretty fast.

CH: Maybe Bernie Leadon and I weren’t as charismatic, or had the focus Gram had when he was on — but by then he was *not* on. The last year before we fired him was really embarrassing, pathetic. There are these guys — little flames that just burn out. But again, Barry — this was his choice. When substance abuse takes over, in music, or the acting world, or anywhere, it’s not a disease in a physiological sense — it’s a disease of selfishness. It becomes more important than your friends. I loved him dearly, and he was so much fun — when the drugs weren’t consuming him, or he them. Dwight [Yoakam], after reading about all that, understood the situation immediately — that we were like brothers. We *were* like brothers — only my brother stabbed me in the back!

ND: Which had to have been a bigger letdown than it would have been otherwise.

CH: Yeah — like Cain and Abel. He *killed* me emotionally, and killed my love for him, by the way he treated me and everybody else in the band.

ND: You say that it was about twenty years before you saw those experiences from this perspective you have today — including your own role and responsibility for the band’s fate. How did you come to put it all in context for yourself that way?

CH: I grew up. I’d been working in a business you didn’t have to grow up in — but then in about 1979 or ’80, after Souther-Hillman-Furay, I did. I never had put myself in harm’s way, at least, and a lot of that has to do with the way I was brought up. I would goof around and try things, but I never would up in the gutter having sold my instruments to buy drugs, or any of that. I just didn’t go that far with it all. But, at 64, I don’t mean to beat myself up over these things. ...There are things I regret, but obviously I was supposed to do those things to get to where I am, to make weird turns and to work with these people I’ve dearly loved.

I wish Gram was alive right now — and I want everybody to know that.

Dwight Yoakam’s a very good friend of mine, and I’ve always looked at him as what Gram *could have been*. Dwight worked really hard at what he did; he created an image and wrote the songs and found songs and is one of the few musicians who can pull it off on screen, too; he’s a good actor.

ND: The Burritos story was, of course, not just about Gram Parsons. Which fellow members, in all the lineups of the band that you were part of, do you consider to have been underestimated, in terms of their contributions?

CH: Gosh, I think Al Perkins was a phenomenal steel player. I think Rick Roberts — who was never really meant to replace Gram; he wasn’t a Gram Parsons — was a very good journeyman singer. He was professional onstage and he did his job. Obviously, he went on and did something else [Firefall], which was not my kind of music, but I had great respect for him. And Bernie Leadon was somebody I could always depend on. I would hold out those three guys as being members of the band in different incarnations who were really good. That’s why I hold up *The*

Last Of The Red Hot Burritos album, really; that was the band, at the very end, that was cookin' when we were playing live. And I loved Michael Clarke, you know; Michael was a soulmate and pal from the Byrds.

ND: One thing that struck me in the book is how much the use of steel guitar — how much and what style — affected the acceptance and the evolution of the music you were making. The handoff from the ace Lloyd Green with the Byrds, then to Sneaky Pete, then to Al Perkins, is a more important part of the story than I'd considered.

CH: Sneaky fit the Burrito Brothers well — because here we were, really coming out of left field, approaching the music from such a strange place, and there's no other steel player that would have worked at the time; he was just eccentric enough to make it work. We weren't ready for Al yet; that was a year and a half away, for when we'd gotten a little more aware of the deficiencies in our execution. Pete had to do all the leads until Bernie came in on guitar, but that's what made it so interesting. There were moments that were great, but there were others that were just unbelievably bad.

Chris Hillman and friends, warming up in the green room at McCabe's, Santa Monica, California. Photograph by Roman Cho.

Sneaky would get so angry because it was all *so* loose. Yet he would never tune and he'd be out of tune himself. He was an interesting guy, because all the steel players I've ever known have been very precise, very anal with their instruments, with everything very precisely in tune and everything working like clockwork. But for Sneaky, whose real job was being a stop motion animator [for the *Gumby* films] which required a very precise kind of mindset, steel was goof-off time! He could be brilliant, and sometimes he could be, well, almost a Lawrence Welk band reject.

ND: The influence of Buck Owens and the Everly Brothers on the Burritos is often noted, but didn't your own bluegrass background have some effect too? By the time of *Last Of The Red Hot*, there was outright bluegrass section of the show. And it's interesting that J.D. Crowe with Doyle Lawson or the Rice Brothers was about the first to cover Burrito songs — "Sin City," "Devil In Disguise," "God's Own Singer."

CH: Oh; that's true. J.D. *was* the first to do that. "My Uncle" is a good example of what was basically a bluegrass song in a straight "two" rhythm — and "Juanita" could have been done as

the Desert Rose Band and written them." — Chris Hillman

a bluegrass ballad, too. We'd already gone there with "Time Between" in the Byrds; I'd known Clarence White since I was 16, and he takes a solo on that track and it's just unbelievable.

ND: It struck me that when bluegrass greats Jim & Jesse recorded that key song for you, Buck's "Under Your Spell Again," with the Grand Ole Opry honky-tonk band for their CD *Our Kind Of Country*, that bluegrass/honky-tonk mix was in some key ways the closest thing I've heard anywhere else to the Burritos sound.

CH: I think so; yeah. They just had it a little more together!

ND: In the wider story of your musical career — and maybe you'll tell that someday — where does the Flying Burrito Brothers adventure fit? I know you've done book interviews about the Byrds, but there's maybe some irony in the fact that, with all you've done, this short story is what comes up for a book now.

CH: You know, my musical redemption came when I'd already had hits with the Desert Rose Band and written them. Talk about consistency in a band; in our heyday we were smokin'. Then I played at Buck Owens' 70th birthday party at his club, with Herb Pedersen. I'll never forget that I walked offstage, and Buck grabbed my arm and said, "Chris, you are one hell of a *singer.*" Can you see what that meant to me? I'd gone for some years just not being a very good one, and I got this approval from a great singer — and that was worth more than anything in the world. Herb and I also worked for him a week before he passed away, and that was real special.

If I remember everything, I'll probably write some memoirs when I get to my 70s — just to recall how funny so much of it all was, and the interesting characters that I've worked with. I've had a good time. And I'm lucky, I guess. There's some reason that I'm not a statistic.

Barry Mazor is a senior editor at NoDepression.com and a frequent contributor to The Wall Street Journal *on country and pop. His book* Meeting Jimmie Rodgers: How America's Original Roots Music Hero Changed The Pop Sounds Of A Century, *will be published by Oxford University Press in May 2009.*

A CONVERSATION WITH JASON RINGENBERG ABOUT JASON & THE SCORCHERS

by DON MCLEESE
photograph by C. TYLER CROTHERS
(and mistreated by SHOCKO GRAFIX)

The musical revolution that we now call alt-country, insurgent country, Americana, whatever, had its Boston Tea Party in Nashville, Tennessee, where Jason Ringenberg, the son of an Illinois hog farmer, moved on July 4, 1981, with the goal of becoming a star. He quickly joined forces with fellow visionary Jack Emerson, who would manage and record Jason & the Nashville Scorchers for his Praxis label, after initially serving as bassist for the fledgling band. Jason would subsequently and crucially recruit bassist Jeff Johnson, guitarist Warner Hodges and drummer Perry Baggs — three punk-rockers who thought country-rock was the squarest thing in the world.

And at the time it was, for the noble (if self-destructive) influence of Gram Parsons and the Flying Burrito Brothers had degenerated into the parody of the New Riders Of The Purple Sage, the "Truckin'" of the Grateful Dead, and the "Peaceful Easy Feeling" of the Eagles and Firefall (both initially featuring Burrito alums). The lame country-rock of the 1970s would become the lamer commercial country of a quarter-century later, but Jason & the Nashville Scorchers had no interest in finding a place in that world. They wanted to put a blowtorch to it.

In the process, they became one of the most incendiary live bands that American music has known, though they never achieved the commercial success that was their due. Perhaps it was because they were ahead of their time, with no context for what they were doing, no Americana category that likely wouldn't exist without the seminal influence of the Scorchers. When they disbanded in 1989, they felt like failures. Jason then became a landscaper, a solo artist and a children's artist (as Farmer Jason).

Yet Jason & the Scorchers refuse to die. The good news for fans is that the band is primed to record its first album of new material in more than a decade. And wherever they play, they'll tear up the joint.

NO DEPRESSION: Let's bring readers up to date. What can you tell us about the new album?

JASON RINGENBERG: When we got the Americana Music Association Lifetime Achievement Award [for performance, in 2008], that was sort of the impetus to think about recording again. But a lot of things have come together this past year. We did a short run through Europe last May and have a really crackin' rhythm section. That's been the weakness, the last ten years, 'cause it's really hard to replace Perry Baggs and Jeff Johnson, I'll tell ya. And we hadn't really done that. But the guys we worked with last spring, we hit a good vibe, and Warner's playing great. And I just kind of have this sort of window between all the other things I'm doing. So we're doing a record this spring.

ND: Who is the rhythm section?

JR: Al Collins is on bass. He's a Nashville guy, and plays with the Stacie Collins Band; he's her

Jason Ringenberg and Warner Hodges at the Ryman Auditorium (with Perry Baggs and Jeff Johnson), celebrating their AMA Lifetime Achievement Award, September 2008. Photograph by Deone Jahnke.

husband and bandleader. And on drums we have Pontus Snibb. Believe it or not, he's a southern boy — from southern Sweden! We did the European tour with him, and he's a young guy, real strong, really muscular player. Which is important for the Scorchers. And he sings great, real musical guy. So we finally found somebody who could stand in Perry's shoes, and we had to go to Sweden to do it.

ND: How are Jeff and Perry doing?

JR: Jeff has essentially retired from music. He's in the film business. He's worked on some big films over the years and he's making his own independent film now. Perry's health is challenging. He has severe diabetes and kidney failure and all the related problems.

ND: So it's now 27 years since the Scorchers originally came together. What's different now?

JR: Well, the entire music business has just changed so radically. I think it has changed more in the last five years than it had the previous 25. It's so much more DIY now, and there are so many more options and availabilities to get your music out. At the same time, it means you're competing with anybody who can play a guitar (laughs). Anybody who can hum a tune can get a CD out nowadays.

ND: Are you looking for a deal or are you going to put the music out yourself?

JR: We're just gonna record it and see what happens. We don't have any record company that's funding the process.

ND: OK, let's go back to ancient history. Why did you move to Nashville?

JR: I came to Nashville to become a star (laughs). That was it. There was nothing else to it. At the time I was living in southern Illinois which is sort of in the Nashville orbit. And it just seemed like an easy step. I had graduated from college and I'd played in bands there and had taken it about as far as I could. I wanted to take another step, and Nashville just seemed the obvious choice. Although I did think about Austin, Memphis and Los Angeles, but Nashville seemed easier.

Ancient history: Jason Ringenberg (far right) with the Catalinas, 1980. Photograph by Scott Nelson.

ND: You had gone to Southern Illinois University in Carbondale?

JR: I graduated with a degree in University Studies (laughs). And if you ask me what that means, I can't tell you. But it's a Bachelor of Science degree, and it's for people who take 120 credit hours and just study what they want to study. And the music I was making was some sort of antecedent to what the Scorchers did, but not nearly as good. There was some country and rootsy sort of stuff

There was nothing else to it." — *Jason Ringenberg*

in the bands I was in. I played in a rockabilly band. And some of it was just covers of whatever was going on at the time.

ND: What were your musical experiences before going to Carbondale?

JR: They were all sort of folkie guy with the harmonica holder. I started seriously when I was about 17, playing acoustic guitar and singing at parties and writing songs. I didn't really think about bands until I was 20 or 21. My dad had always had the local AM country stations on, because they gave the farm reports. Weather and commodity prices. So that was always on, the AM radio in his '68 Chevy truck. But I also had older siblings who were '60s kids, so they turned me on to Dylan and Neil Young and The Band and Creedence, those sort of people. I might listen to David

Bowie, but I always ended back in that country-rock world. I was a huge Ozark Mountain Daredevils fan, for example. Nuts about that band. Still am. And of course, Jerry Lee [Lewis] was huge in my world. As a performer, Jerry Lee was the prototype. He was the template.

ND: So, when you get to Nashville, did you have this idea of Jason & the Nashville Scorchers in your head? Or did you have any idea how you planned to become a star?

JR: I didn't know. Fate was with me. God was traveling in that old Econline van, because I just started driving around Nashville. And I had nothing. I knew no one. I had no money. And I had all my stuff, the whole of my civilization was in that old white van. I drove around, and I found this little place for rent, and I got it. And it just so happened it was right behind the only original music club in Nashville, Cantrell's. *Right* behind it. And I had no idea what Cantrell's was. That very night I moved in, I heard this music coming from there, and I went over and started hanging out. And the next night, R.E.M. played there. This little band from Athens, in their little green Dodge van. And I got to know people from hanging out. The first one was Jack Emerson, and he was the catalyst for everything.

ND: How crucial was Jack in the band's development?

JR: I would not be in the music business if it hadn't been for Jack Emerson [who died of a heart attack in 2003].

Nashville punks (l. to r.), 1982: Warner Hodges, Perry Baggs, Jason Ringenberg, and Jeff Johnson. Photograph by Anita French.

And there would never have been a Jason & the Scorchers. There was kind of a sister club to Cantrell's, run by the same people but much smaller. I met Jack there, just a week or so after getting to Nashville. I was just shaking hands with everybody I could, saying, "I want to be a legend. I want to make this supercharged American music, rock 'n' roll meets punk-rock. Can you help me? Do you know anybody?" I'd talk to *anybody* about this. Jack was in this club, and there was a Sex Pistols cover band, so there were all these poseurs hanging out. They thought I was the squarest guy ever. I had a bolo tie on and a plaid shirt and a straw hat. They all had their haircuts and leather jackets. But Jack got it immediately. He said this was a great idea. And on the spot, one minute into the conversation, he said, "I'll help you with this! In fact, I have a bass guitar and I'll even learn how to play a little until you find a good band." And he did it! He found

Jason Ringenberg at the Cat's Pajamas, East Nashville, Tennessee, 2004. Photograph by David Wilds.

a drummer and a guitar player, and he played a little bass. Very little, I should say. And we did a few shows. Got a gig opening for Carl Perkins and another opening for R.E.M. And those shows are where Warner and Jeff saw me and everything started to fall into place.

ND: Was the original band billed as Jason & the Nashville Scorchers?

JR: Yes, there was a Jason & the Nashville Scorchers before Warner, Jeff and Perry. The drummer, Barry Felts, passed away a long time ago from drugs. The guitar player, Will Tomlinson, is an attorney in California. And then Jack played bass. As it became evident that that band was as far as I could take it, a few months into it, Jeff was the first one I met. He said he wanted to jump in and help. He was a guitar player, but he said he'd play bass, and he took over Jack's spot. We kept Barry, and Will quit or something, so Jeff said, "Let me try Warner. I know he *can* play it. The question is whether he *will* play it." Jeff and Warner were friends, but Barry hated Warner Hodges. Barry was a good drummer and charismatic and a good singer, but I just had this instinctive feeling about Warner. Though everybody in town told me not to play with him. Said he was nothing but trouble. He had an absolute reputation. And Jeff was right with him in the reputation category. They were twins in the same sort of world — heavy experiences in the mythical world of rock 'n' roll. You had to destroy yourself to be a rocker, and they burned a lot of bridges. They drank a lot of peoples' beer.

ND: But you thought you could make it work?

JR: Yeah, I had this feeling, and then when I heard Warner play, it was like, *Oh boy, this is really good.* And I was able to keep Barry Felts on for one gig. It was in November of '81, and we played this little college punk-rock club, and it was just amazing! It was so explosive. And me and Warner and Jeff just jumped off the stage saying that was the coolest gig we've ever done. And Barry said, "That was the worst S-H-I-T I have ever played on. I quit!" And so he quit.

it was more like an explosion." — *Jason Ringenberg*

And Warner said, "I have a drummer friend named Perry Baggs." And he said the same thing that Jeff had said about Warner. "I don't know if he *will* do it, but I know he *can* do it." So Warner brought in Perry and we set up in my little shotgun shack in West Nashville. We played "Gone, Gone, Gone" by Carl Perkins, and from the first measure I knew that this was the band that was going to do it. I think the walls were melting almost from the intensity of the chemistry. That first rehearsal, it wasn't a rehearsal, it was more like an explosion.

ND: Prior to you guys getting together, from the time of Gram Parsons through the '70s, country-

Nashville Skyline (l. to r.), 1996: Jason Ringenberg, Perry Baggs, Jeff Johnson, and Warner Hodges. Photograph by Jim Herrington.

rock had gotten kind of a reputation of being mellow, laid-back, whatever. Did you connect with that side of country-rock, or did you think you were doing something totally different?

JR: Well, I know the other guys in the band wanted nothing to do with country-rock. They thought it was the squarest thing possible. And in fact, despite my own roots in country-rock and my love of it, the Scorchers had very little to do with it. We were a punk-rock band from the south. We were anti-country-rock, really. If anybody even breathed that word around us, they got their head cut off.

ND: So you wouldn't have admitted that you loved the Ozark Mountain Daredevils?

JR: Not to Warner Hodges.

ND: Since your formative influ-

ences were more toward what we now call classic rock and country, how did you develop the affinity for punk?

JR: I listened to some of the Pistols and the Ramones back in Illinois, but it really was Warner who brought that to the party in a big way. And Jeff's sense of rhythm, right out of the Dee Dee Ramone songbook.

ND: So was this band a matter of kindred spirits or opposites attracting? Or spontaneous combustion?

JR: Certainly spontaneous combustion and opposites attracting. We had nothing in common. Musically speaking, Warner really hated Bob Dylan. He wished Bob Dylan was dead, at the time.

And I could have cared less about [AC/DC guitarist] Angus Young. We fought all the time. Me and Warner to a point, but there was plenty among the rest. We were a very volatile band. I can't remember a single time when there was somebody not mad at somebody about something. The *only* time it would work was on the good shows, when we walked onstage and everything clicked. It was pure magic. And then we'd walk offstage and find something to argue about.

ND: Early on, what sort of clubs did you play and what kind of audiences did you draw?

JR: People would think that we came out of honky-tonks, but we didn't. There was no way at that time that a band like the Scorchers could exist in the country world. The few times we played honky-tonks or country clubs were absolute disasters. We had our best success in punk-rock clubs. Or what was called new wave at the time. The trendy new wavers never got us, but people like Steve Earle did. Though we did have some very successful shows at the Danceteria, a new wave dance club in New York.

Jason & the Nashville Scorchers, 1983. Photographer unknown.

ND: Did the Nashville music community feel like you were making fun of country music?

JR: Some did, but not as many as you might think. Especially in the Nashville music business world, a lot of people were curious about the band, even excited. Jerry Crutchfield, who was Lee Greenwood's producer and would later produce my solo record, would hang out at the Scorchers' shows, and he was a major Music Row producer. Rodney Crowell was into the band. Bill Golden from the Oak Ridge Boys jammed with us a few times. Billy Ray Cyrus in his early days got into the band. A lot of people thought the band was the coolest thing, because pretty much everybody has a gripe against Music Row at one point in their life or another. And the Scorchers were so anti-Music Row, so many Nashville people could relate to us.

ND: But if you were anti-Music Row, you weren't anti-Nashville, right?

JR: We were only anti-'80s Music Row. Perry grew up listening to great country and gospel music, and Jeff had never had a problem with country music, the real stuff. And Warner too, he was a big Merle Haggard fan. But we all hated what country music had become. That was the one thing we all agreed on 100 percent.

ND: You were early on saddled with the category "cowpunk." What did you think of that?

JR: We virulently hated it and fought it every step of the way. But looking back, I guess that's what we were. We just said we were an American rock 'n' roll band.

find something to argue about." — *Jason Ringenberg*

ND: People from the start would comment on the difference between your polite, gentlemanly offstage demeanor and your livewire, crazed intensity onstage. How do you account for those differences, and do you see these as two different personalities?

JR: I'm a natural performer I guess. I just love to perform and always have, since I was a child. It's just that release, though I've never been able to figure it out. Or how it turns on. I've become a little better at being able to turn it on and off, but it's something that just clicks when I step onto that stage. A different personality takes hold.

ND: Do you feel like a different person when you're onstage?

JR: I do completely. It's not something I think about. It's all *now*. And it's either working or it isn't.

ND: When you started playing beyond Nashville, was the response different?

JR: We were so audacious, Jack Emerson and myself. It was like, "OK, we have a band, let's put it on the road." So it wasn't like we played a lot in Nashville and then moved it out. As soon as *Reckless Country Soul* came out, which was in January of '82, only a few weeks into the band being what it was with Perry, we were playing shows all over the south. I don't know how we did this, but we were able to talk people into booking us. But to answer your question, I don't think there was a huge difference. There was an added chemistry in Nashville, because it was our hometown and the home of country music. But everywhere we played, you had people hungry for something different but who still loved organic music. And that was our fan base around the country.

ND: Early on, the band was known for playing a lot of covers. How'd you choose which songs to play?

JR: Looking back, I don't think we were all that original, but we did a lot of cool stuff. I remember "Candy Kisses" we did, and "I'd Rather Die Young," the old Johnny Cash song, and we just gave 'em all the same treatment, throw eighth-notes on them and holler as loud as we could. At

EMI recording artists Jason, Perry, Jeff, and Warner. Photograph by Peter Nash.

the time, it was absolutely revolutionary. People were stunned. The energy just overwhelmed the intellectual analysis.

ND: "Absolutely Sweet Marie" was a breakthrough. Did you bring that to the band?

JR: Yes, I did. I was listening heavily to that one side of *Blonde On Blonde,* and I could just hear what Jeff particularly would do with that song. And I knew Warner would be great, but I didn't play them the record, because Warner of course hated Bob Dylan. He couldn't even spell Bob Dylan at the time. So I said here's a cool song, and I just sang it. And we'd already had *Fervor* out with

Jack's label [Praxis] and we did that first tour of California, which changed our lives. All of a sudden we went from this little hillbilly outfit to having the biggest labels in the world after us. All in one two-week tour. And when we got signed to EMI, they said we want this out in January, but we need something to make *Fervor* different. So we recorded "Absolutely Sweet Marie." Looking back at how fast things happened in those days, I remember doing that L.A. tour in early December of '83 and the video was playing on MTV in early January. Amazing.

ND: Why'd you decide to sign with EMI, and how did a major-label contract change things?

JR: We had our choice of just about everybody. It was an amazing thing. We couldn't afford duct tape, and here when we get to Los Angeles, we have Chrysalis and A&M and CBS and everybody, and all of them were just fawning over the band. All we had to do was get them out [to the shows] and they followed like a herd, and all of them made offers. And we got a huge deal. We really liked EMI's A&R people a lot, and in retrospect I think it was a pretty good decision.

ND: Were they the ones who wanted you to drop "Nashville" from the Scorchers?

JR: That was purely the label's idea, and it's the one thing in my life that I'm consistently ashamed of. I wish we wouldn't have done that. 'Cause I thought that was the coolest name, Jason & the Nashville Scorchers. Though when the label suggested it, I figured it was just a word, no big deal. But boy were our fans infuriated. They didn't understand it. Nor should they have. And I regretted it almost immediately. To this day I regret it.

ND: The music you made for EMI and Praxis is considered classic at this point. But it consistently fared better with critics and live audiences than it did with radio and record stores. Was that a frustrating situation for the band?

JR: Oh, yes, absolutely. And it eventually led to the first breakup in the late '80s. The results never remotely matched the expectations for the band. Our own expectations, the record company's, the people around the band.

A&M recording artists (l. to r.): Andy York, Perry Baggz [sic], Ken Fox, Jason Ringenberg, and Warner Hodges. Photograph by Peter Nash.

Even in Nashville, the Scorchers never broke out of clubs and into theaters. It was very difficult.

ND: When you consider that all these labels had been chasing you and must have thought you had commercial potential, what went wrong? 'Cause it couldn't have been the music — the music's strong.

JR: I believe so. But to make the Scorchers a hit act, I'm not sure that ever was in the cards. I think if it hadn't been for certain marketing decisions or bad luck, we could have gotten as big as Steve Earle or Los Lobos — on that level. And we never really did. But overall, since we've been able to still make records and people still care about us, there's no sense going on about it too much.

the expectations for the band." — Jason Ringenberg

ND: Was the response different in Europe?

JR: It was, but not really to the level of the urban legend that surrounds it. We were never stars in Europe. But we had more success in Europe than we had in the States, and we still do.

ND: At the start it seemed like you were the only ones doing what you were doing. By the time you signed with EMI, and through the mid-'80s, were there artists and acts who you considered kindred spirits?

JR: The two bands I remembered from the very early days were Rank And File and Lone Justice, and we were all playing the same circuit and compared in reviews to each other. In fact, I think the first Scorchers gig in L.A. was opening for Lone Justice. And we were aware of Dwight [Yoakam], too. And Steve Earle. And Los Lobos. And Joe Ely, of course. But it was a pretty short list.

ND: And none of them were as punk as you were, even though Rank And File had come out of that.

JR: Exactly. We were a punk-rock band.

ND: After two albums with EMI, there was an extended interval, a new label, a new album, and then an extended hiatus. What happened?

JR: We never thought of it as a hiatus. We broke up after *Thunder And Fire*. And Jeff had left right before *Thunder And Fire*. Again, it was the same thing. A&M signed us to this gigantically huge recording contract. I can't believe they would do that. We'd never had a hit! And the record came out [in 1989] and nothing happened! It was by far the worst release we had in the '80s in terms of commercial reception. We were literally like a three-week promotional campaign. The record came out, we did a tour and then it was over. And

Still Scorching: live, but undated. Photograph by Chris Eselgroth.

after we'd spent two years recording the record and a huge amount of money. And then nothing happens. And Perry comes down with diabetes, ends up in the hospital. Warner says he can't do this anymore. A&M drops us. And we just fell apart.

ND: Critically, *Thunder And Fire* didn't get much of a response. Did you consider this a much different album? Were you disappointed with it?

JR: You know, I believe it was one of our finer records, and over the years a lot of fans have rediscovered it. At the time, yeah, it wasn't received well. But I liked it at the time. I certainly think it's way better than *Still Standing* and probably better than *A Blazing Grace*.

ND: Well, *Thunder And Fire* is often considered the album where Warner had the most input. Is that the correct impression?

JR: Absolutely. And also the five-piece band changed things quite a bit. Andy York [second guitarist] is a major musician, and he influenced it for the better. And Barry Beckett's production was actually quite good. But, yeah, it's a big rock record, no doubt about it.

ND: So then you fell apart, broke up, whatever. And you were mowing lawns during that time?

JR: Yeah, that's what I was doing. I put together a deal with Capitol, but man, it was really slow going. They gave me no money, no support, and Jerry Crutchfield was my only ally at the label. So I didn't have a band and I didn't have a clue. How does Jason live in the music world without the Scorchers? And it was a bad time, all the way around, personally too. So I made the one record, but yeah, I was working as a landscaper.

ND: And then you got back together with the band in the mid-'90s.

JR: Jeff really got into the *Essential* re-release [on CD] of *Fervor* and *Lost And Found*, and he started calling us. He was really persistent. And I wanted nothing to do with it. I had absolutely no desire to be a Scorcher again. And Warner really didn't either. But what Jeff would do is call me up and say, "Hey, Warner's really into this. Come on!" And he'd call Warner and say, "Jason's really into this!" And so we put together a few reunion dates and got paid a lot of money and had a lot of fun. And it just seemed like there was something there. And in fact there was. While we'd been gone, alt-country had happened and everyone was pointing to the Scorchers as an antecedent of that. And people were having real success, Uncle Tupelo and the Bottle Rockets and all of them claiming the Scorchers as ancestors of it. And fans checking us out; all of a sudden there were young people at our shows.

ND: Why had you resisted?

Warner Hodges and Jason Ringenberg, 2008. Photograph by Deone Jahnke.

JR: It was just full of bad memories for me, at the time. In 1990-91 the Scorchers just looked like a gigantic failure. To us and really to everyone else. No one in 1991 would have said that Jason & the Scorchers were a legendary band. It took sort of the emergence of the alt-country phenomenon for the Scorchers to regain their place in the music industry world. And once that happened, it was easier to look at the band in a much more positive light. Before that, it just seemed like a big, painful failure.

ND: So, do you feel the band was too far ahead of its time? That things would have been different if you'd come along later?

like a gigantic failure." — *Jason Ringenberg*

JR: I don't know. Some people suggest that. We got a lot of attention because we were so far ahead of our time. It's an exciting thing to be one of the handful of people in the world doing a certain kind of music. If "White Lies" had come out in '86 — when the [Georgia] Satellites came out with "Keep Your Hands To Yourself" — instead of '85, it might have been different. I mean, "Keep Your Hands To Yourself" was a great single, but "White Lies" was a great single, too. If *Lost And Found* had come out a year or two later, things might have been different. Though people make the argument that without *Lost And Found,* there wouldn't have been any of that [roots-rocking alt-country] anyway. That record changed a lot of things.

ND: So, this time through, did you have to be dragged into a reunion or are you enthusiastic about it?

JR: There've been so many reunions (laughs) that I almost hesitate to use that word anymore. There's always been a band doing an occasional show, since 1981. But it has been a long time since we've recorded original material, and I didn't have to be dragged, kicking and screaming. We had a really good time last May, and there were too many things pointing to the fact that we should do another record again.

ND: Are there musical facets that are different when you're fronting the Scorchers than if you're recording as Jason Ringenberg?

JR: The nuts and bolts of it is that Warner Hodges is one of the finest, if not the finest, rock 'n' roll country guitar player ever. So if you don't have that, you're going to miss something. And I do write somewhat differently for myself than I do for the Scorchers, because there are certain rhythm patterns that can work only with Jason & the Scorchers. And that's an advantage, knowing what that band can do. And there are also limitations that I don't have when I'm recording on my own or as Farmer Jason.

ND: This time through, what are your hopes and aspirations for the band?

JR: I don't think we have any pretensions of, *We're gonna make our best record ever!* And I don't have any goals to make a commercial statement. This record actually may only be available at jasonandthescorchers.com. Who knows? But I know there are songs to be written, and I know that Warner Hodges is playing at his peak, some mind-blowing stuff. And for that reason alone, it's time to make a Jason & the Scorchers record.

Jason and the Scorchers got together the year after Don McLeese joined the Chicago Sun-Times *as pop music critic. When Don and Jason realized that they'd had their first interview a quarter-century ago, it made at least one of them feel very, very old.*

This may seem like an odd question, coming

Jeffrey Hatcher's healing

words and photograph by **PAUL CANTIN**

from a music publication, but...is music...

If you don't mind hearing all about me,
Look out, mama, I'm a-hundred-and-three,
And tomorrow don't mean more than yesterday to me
  — Jeffrey Hatcher/David Briggs "Coming To Collect" (1980)

necessary?

In recent years we've seen evidence that just about everything associated with music is up for grabs — how music is made, sold, distributed, promoted, performed, consumed. Despite all the hand-wringing about the state of the music business, music itself endures, as it has survived for centuries. It makes you wonder, is there some basic, human, biological necessity that music fulfills?

vaults over intellectual defenses...

It's a question Jeffrey Hatcher has pondered, too. Hatcher works in Winnipeg, capital of the Canadian province of Manitoba, as a music therapist, helping some of the most troubled and marginalized people — especially young people — deal with the underlying issues in their lives through songwriting. Aspiring gang members, car thieves, drug users, victims of sexual abuse — Hatcher has seen them heal through the simple act of expressing themselves musically, with his trained guidance.

As Hatcher says, there is no magic wand. But it is magic of a sort. It's as if our emotional response to music vaults over intellectual defenses, helping us penetrate to the core issues of our past and unravel the mysteries of our own challenges.

"The experiencing of music bypasses the frontal cortex, the executive processing part of the brain that would otherwise let you decide whether you like this music or not," Hatcher explains. "Instead, the music touches the memory and emotion parts of the brain, namely the amygdala and hippocampus, mysterious organs that are involved with the processing of memory and emotion, leaving us helpless in its thrall."

Technically, that's how music can unite a stadium full of people in common cause, or let a solitary listener experience an emotional epiphany while riding on a bus listening to an iPod. "By inviting the listener in, then the listener inviting the music in further...the dance continues as the person creates the music, creating the experience triggering the memory, stimulating the emotion, and on and on," he says of the music therapy process.

Lest you think, from his technical explanation, that Hatcher is some lab-coated clinician, know this: Hatcher himself is an example of music's durable power. Prior to his current career in music therapy, the 51-year-old singer, songwriter and guitarist had, by some measure, three good swipes at grabbing the showbiz brass ring: first in

Jeffrey Hatcher (at left) singing in 2004 with the Fuse: David Briggs (center) and Don Hatcher. Courtesy Stu Reid. Previous pages, Jeffrey Hatcher (left) and Billy Cowsill perform as the Blue Shadows at the Austin Cantin, 1994.

the late 1970s co-fronting the Fuse, a gritty combo that both predicted and later rode the new wave in rock music; then during the roots-rock insurgency of the early '80s with Jeffrey Hatcher & the Big Beat; and finally alongside fallen '60s teen-idol Bill Cowsill in the Blue Shadows, considered by some to be one of the great lost groups of the alt-country movement.

There are a passel of recordings (many referenced in this article can be heard at www.broadjam.com/hatcherbriggs), some stellar songs, and the fading memory of galvanic live performances to show for those efforts, not to mention a scattered diaspora of true believers who heard and witnessed what might have been and wonder to this day why, in commercial terms, it never really was.

"I thought he would be huge...Hatcher managed to take everything I liked about country music and everything I liked about pop music and put it together effortlessly and seamlessly without being contrived," says Tom Wilson of Blackie & the Rodeo Kings, who recalls in the 1980s nudging his way backstage past headliners to meet opening-act Hatcher. "I thought I could totally see myself in the back of an arena someday trying to see this guy. Jeffrey Hatcher's music spoke the same way. It was big. I wouldn't compare it to Springsteen, but it was that big to me."

When Hatcher managed to get the attention of influential music critics, they concurred. Dave Marsh described Hatcher and company as "a lot more than the best band to come out of Winnipeg since the Guess Who" and "twangy and soulful enough to be dangerous." Anthony DeCurtis called their sound "infectious, upbeat and deeply felt." Toronto's *Globe & Mail* called Hatcher a "genuinely intriguing performer" and declared his songs packed "real emotional resonance."

So why did acclaim fail to translate into widespread commercial fortune? Wilson reckons part of the problem was timing. Hatcher was a prime practitioner of a kind of music that wouldn't find a place in the business until some years later. "He wasn't trying too hard to impress anybody. It just was what it was. Before there was New Country, before there was a stream for people like Buddy Miller and Steve Earle...to me he rode with that crop," he says.

Dark Horse, at their second gig, River Heights Junior High School, Winnipeg, 1977 (l. to r.): David Briggs, Randy Smith, Paul Hatcher, and Jeffrey Hatcher. Photograph courtesy Jeffrey Hatcher.

Vancouver singer Wendy Bird recently recorded a full album of Hatcher originals with assistance from a group of players — including Elvis Costello — who essentially volunteered their time in service to Hatcher's music. "His songs move me," she says. "I can get behind them. I don't have to know the exact meaning of them, but I can relate to them on a certain level. They may seem simple on the surface, but there is usually a deeper perspective....I wish he was more known. He should be. He deserves to be."

For more than a decade, Hatcher has had nothing to do with the music business. But that is not to say he has been estranged from music. In a very real way, his work in music therapy sees him operating more purely as a musician — exploring the fundamental purpose of music in our lives — than ever. Where once he collaborated with fellow musicians and wrote songs hopefully aimed at a broad commercial audience, now he helps create songs intended for an audience of one — his own collaborating clients. And it is fair to say that, for those clients, the songs they produce are more powerful and life-changing than anything that ever gets on the radio or the charts. People talk sentimentally about the healing power of music, but Hatcher lives it every working day.

"It is really gratifying that I did find this," Hatcher says of his work in music therapy. "It was cool to find this thing that was not just a continuation of being a musician, but a real stretch

costumes….People were angry at us." — Jeffrey Hatcher

and really engaging other interests I have: psychology, sociology, anthropology. [Music therapy] kind of threw the whole mess together. I didn't think I would ever find that, anywhere."

He recognizes, though, it makes for an unlikely climax to a career in music.

"It's more like a knight's move on a chessboard — one forward and two sideways."

lthough he has spent spells in Toronto and Vancouver, Hatcher's birthplace and current home is Winnipeg. Located near the longitudinal heart of North America, it's a flat prairie landscape battered by ridiculously harsh winters and summers filled with long, cloudless dry days. Winnipeg has always housed a vibrant art scene. It did indeed spawn the Guess Who, and it was also where Neil Young spent his formative years. More recently, Winnipeg has given the world the Crash Test Dummies, the Weakerthans, techno artist Venetian Snares, and the Duhks. It is also the city for which Winnie-the-Pooh was named.

Hatcher doesn't recall a time when he wasn't drawn to music. "I loved singing with pop music on the radio and folk music," he recalls. "I could instinctively sing harmony, which was really fun. I didn't know everybody couldn't do that." Trawling through a friend's collection of British Invasion 45s fed an interest in pop; early experiments with the trumpet and recorder were replaced by the desire for a guitar, which he received on the occasion of his thirteenth Christmas. When he was 16, the acoustic was replaced by an electric. But as Hatcher moved into his teens and popular music grew increasingly complex, self-serious and heavy, he was already a young man out of time. While his contemporaries were genuflecting at Zeppelin and Humble Pie, Hatcher was enthralled by the *American Graffiti* soundtrack.

"I didn't know anyone who liked the music I liked," he says. "I didn't know anyone who was playing guitar. Musicians I did know were playing piano and reading, not playing by ear. So I was on my own." But not for long. His piano-playing pal Dave Briggs switched to guitar, and the pair absorbed the Buddy Holly, Chuck Berry, Beatles and Stones songbooks. Hatcher's younger brother Paul joined in on drums, and with a rotating cast of bassists and occasional keyboardists (that door would revolve throughout their career), they performed their first gig in 1976 at their junior high school dance as the Boys. The next year, they returned to the same venue as Dark Horse. Eventually, they settled on the name the Fuse.

They were initially met with indifference or incomprehension or hostility. "We must have looked like some folk act with electric instruments," he recalls. "We looked completely unremarkable and we weren't impressed by lights or costumes. We just got up there and played songs. People were angry at us."

But something was happening. In New York and London, the musical insurgency that was first called punk and later new wave began to break out. It was a rising tide in musical fashion that inadvertently carried the Fuse to new heights. Overnight, it was like the inside joke that the Hatchers and Briggs had been sharing was suddenly common cause with music fans in their hometown. "Within about four weeks, suddenly some ice broke. We were playing around and then suddenly the places were full." While they held down steady weeknight bar gigs, the group exploited a hole in Manitoba liquor licensing laws and began to organize socials, which were more like full-blown concert events.

(In Manitoba, socials are ticketed, licensed events that individuals are permitted to hold for charitable purposes, such as fundraising events for sports teams or to help fund an engaged couple. Traditionally, live music is part of the deal, but over time the music became the tail that wagged the dog, and enterprising bands like the Fuse would find a soccer club or a couple willing to at least temporarily lend their credibility to weekend recreation.)

In 1978 and 1979, the band played around 30 or 40 full weeks per year, plus plenty of one-nighters. Their sound clenched like a fist. Hatcher's younger brother Don would eventually join, first on bass, later on guitar and sax, and Hatcher

The Fuse, 1979 promotional photograph (l. to r.): Jeffrey Hatcher, Don and Paul Hatcher, and David Briggs.

and Briggs became a potent songwriting team. "I remember going from a small, scrappy band with good ideas, to an effective scrappy band with focused ideas in just a few months," Hatcher says. They recorded an EP that included his song "Writing On The Wall," which presented lyrical compression and cocksure wit with a bullish faith in velocity for its own sake.

> *You better get used to crying tears,*
> *He'll never change in a million years,*
> *Hey don't you know he's a waste of your time,*
> *And now you're borrowing mine*

A handful of live recordings from that era confirm the Fuse was a tight, loud, stripped-down outfit that could summon near-pandemonium in its audience. Greatness was confidently predicted by local partisans, a faith that received an unlikely benediction from Elvis Costello. When he passed through Winnipeg on his tour for *This Year's Model*, he went to catch the Fuse's show. A jam session resulted. There were suggestions the British singer was interested in working further with the group, possibly as producer. But the zeal of that night did not translate into concrete plans. Likewise, the regional momentum the group generated did not convert into broader success. They were kings at home. But there was nowhere to go.

After an eighteen-month estrangement, Briggs and Jeffrey and Paul Hatcher regrouped

a faith that received an unlikely benediction from Elvis Costello.

in Toronto and recorded an album as the Six, which included what would become one of the combo's signature songs, Hatcher's "World Radio." It's Horatio Alger filtered through Chuck Berry — a guitar-slinging immigrant arrives in New York, plugs in and sets the world alight ("That's the way that the story goes/Manhattan fell like dominoes"). But undercutting the optimism was this sobering refrain:

> *I'm always trying for something, that's all there is to it*
> *Trying must count for something, 'cause dying don't count for shit*

But Toronto proved to be cliquey and more self-consciously preoccupied with hipness than Winnipeg, where the group's lack of gimmickry was an asset, not a liability. In 1984, Briggs quit (although he continued to collaborate with the group), Don Hatcher rejoined his brothers in Toronto, and they renamed themselves the Jackals, then later Jeffrey Hatcher & the Big Beat. Now the songwriting and leadership role was squarely on Jeffrey's shoulders, and the frustrations of that time began to infect the new songs.

"For 99 years they're sailing along/Driving up river, selling their song," Hatcher howled on "99 Years." "Poor boy he never learned no better/Poor boy he never learned to bow/He never did buy that story/He's never gonna buy it now." In hindsight, it's easy to see the songs as both autotherapy, intended to balm feelings frazzled by rejection and delay, and a self-administered pep talk to persevere.

One night during that period, Hatcher was fooling around with a Creedence-like guitar part. "This picture came to me," he says, "of someone being out on the road, not being sure if they should have gone out on their own, not being sure where to go. But they just keep going. That's a pretty common showbiz story. But there was something melancholy and powerful about it." The song became "Deliver Me," one of the most enduring of Hatcher's career — a dark-night-of-the-soul confessional with a

The Big Beat (l. to r.): Jeffrey, Don, and Paul Hatcher, at an in-store event. Photograph courtesy Stu Reid.

powerful lyric that's almost hymnlike in its simplicity: "Deliver me from my yesterdays/Hold us together if it can't be done/Deliver me from all that might be/If we get what we want."

"Deliver Me" would anchor a four-song indie EP the Big Beat issued in 1986, and once again they appeared poised to catch a pop-culture wave. Groups such as X, the Blasters and Los

Lobos were stirring a renewed interest in what some were calling "roots rock." Both Warner Bros. and Columbia in New York began flirting with the band; interest from the U.S. naturally triggered belated notice in Canada. Ultimately, they ended up with the indie Upside Records (and CBS in Canada). The Cars' guitarist Elliott Easton was drafted to prepare remixes of "Deliver Me" and "99 Years." Another track, a jaunty, sly political metaphor titled "The Man Who Would Be King," was feted with a video heavily aired in Canada, and it all served to make the LP, *Cross Our Hearts*, a modest hit. The group toured across Canada and played a memorable

gig at the original Lone Star Cafe in New York City during a music conference in 1987. Things were looking up.

Although Hatcher continued to develop as a songwriter and he demoed some stellar material for a follow-up, there were problems with a new management team, and the resulting album would never see the light of day. Even as the band was disintegrating, Hatcher received an overture to sign with another label, but declined. "There was no band here anymore. Forget it. We owed a bunch of money [for the making of the album] and we just paid it back."

In late 1990, Hatcher's partner, the artist Leah Decter, planned to study in Vancouver, so the couple relocated there, although Hatcher's future plans were wide open. "I wasn't sure if I had another band in me or not," he says.

It so happened that Rosanne Cash was performing in Vancouver, and Hatcher (via an old contact with her manager) convinced the promoter to let him open the show as a solo act, but he could not rent a guitar without a refer-

The Big Beat, 1987 (l. to r.): Don Hatcher, Paul Hatcher, Gord Girvan, Jeffrey Hatcher, and Steve Vickery. Courtesy Stu Reid.

ence from a fellow musician. Hatcher dialed his pal, guitarist Danny Casavant, who vouched for him. During the conversation, Casavant casually mentioned he was about to leave a local group. Perhaps Hatcher was interested in taking on his spot with Billy Cowsill?

Some weeks later, Hatcher was finishing a Vancouver club gig with Cowsill when, for reasons never identified, an ornery patron approached Cowsill and expressed both his displeasure with the singer and his desire to settle the matter with fisticuffs. Cowsill responded by picking up his acoustic guitar and hammering the fellow's head.

"Billy gave him a wood shampoo with a Takamine," recalls Cowsill's manager, Dave Chesney. "Laid him out on the dance floor and they dragged him out by his boot heels and dumped him in the street."

and even harder to exaggerate the ups and downs of his tumultuous life.

Hatcher told Chesney and his management partner, Larry Wanagas, that he was alarmed. Was this going to be a regular feature of his new life as sideman to Cowsill? The managers assured the new guitarist that the incident was totally out of character. You could gig with Billy Cowsill for 100 years and something like that will never happen again. Reassured, Hatcher returned for the next night's performance. Like clockwork, a friend of the previous night's victim came after Cowsill hellbent on payback, with predictable results.

"Billy coco-bonked him, too," Chesney says. "Two nights, two guitars."

It would be hard to contain the full life of William Cowsill Jr. within these pages, and even harder to exaggerate the ups and downs of his tumultuous life. Born in 1948 in Middletown, Rhode Island, Cowsill was the eldest member of the singing family band known as the Cowsills. Considered by some the quintessential bubblegum group of the late '60s and early '70s, the Cowsills earned an indelible spot in pop history with the million-selling "The Rain, The Park And Other Things." Although the siblings (and also mom Barbara) sang, it was big brother Bill who performed lead on that signature song. (Singer-songwriter Susan Cowsill was the group's tambourine-banging youngest member.) The group served as the model for "The Partridge Family" TV series; David Cassidy's character was modeled on Bill. Other chart songs would follow, along with numerous TV appearances, tours, and a milk marketing campaign built around their wholesome looks.

But Bill chafed at the group's teenybopper image, and after he was caught smoking pot in 1969, he was fired from the group and (as Bill often joked) booted from the family. He fell in with a coterie of Los Angeles musicians, including Waddy Wachtel and Warren Zevon, and was subsequently asked to sub for Brian Wilson on tour with the Beach Boys; Cowsill said he turned the gig down after being warned off by a then-bedbound Brian. (In 2000, I asked Zevon about his relationship with Cowsill. Zevon was silent for about ten seconds and then answered in a flat, unreadable tone: "I knew him." Next question...)

The Cowsills, on the cover of their album Captain Sad & His Ship Of Fools, *ca. 1968.*

Cowsill set out on an odyssey that took him to Tulsa, where he played with J.J. Cale. Then to Greenwich Village, where he ran with Joe Ely (Chesney says Cowsill claimed he and Ely traveled with an heiress named Peaches to visit Buddy Holly's grave in Lubbock). Then Austin, where Cowsill was part of the scene at a bar called McNeil Depot (now called Donn's Depot), and then back to Los Angeles where he worked for a time as a session musician. In 1971, he cut an eccentric pop album for MGM entitled *Nervous Breakthrough*, which failed to break through.

He drifted up to Canada and made his living gigging with country acts in Alberta, working for a time as a big rig driver on the northern ice highways before relocating to Vancouver and recording with the country-rock band Blue Northern. Then as a solo act, accompanied by upright bassist Elmar Spanier and some occasional side players, he developed a following in western Canada performing the "Dead Guys Set" — covers only by artists who had left this mortal coil.

He was, by some accounts, a deeply troubled soul, but his love of music was undiminished. "Despite his foibles and ups and downs, he always got work," says Chesney. "You could put him in a corner with a guitar and a P.A. and he could go for hours on end. He'd sing Elvis Presley, Roy Orbison, the Beatles. People sat there slack-jawed. There was always that recognition — the fallen star. But nobody really held a lot of pity for Billy unless they dealt with him on a personal level because when he went onstage, he would destroy the place."

"I had heard he was a wild man with a golden voice. And he was all that," Hatcher recalls of meeting Cowsill. "He was funny and savvy. Intelligent. Fun to talk to but erratic; his attention was all over the place. He was kind of crazy but kind-hearted." After the back-to-back guitar-smashing gigs, however, Hatcher was uncertain about their future. "It was brutality. I thought, this guy has horseshoes up his butt. How has he not been killed? It was outrageous behavior."

Elmar Spanier, who played upright bass with the Blue Shadows through recording of their debut album, and Billy Cowsill.

They made for an unlikely pair. Hatcher enjoys a comparatively healthy lifestyle and laid-back demeanor. Rail-skinny Cowsill subsisted on nicotine, caffeine and not much else that was healthy. But they were prepared to forgive each other their differences for one simple reason: They found they could make some great music together. They shared a common love of the sounds of the '50s and '60s. As they began to harmonize together, they locked into a tight, intuitive blend that usually requires shared DNA. Hatcher remembers the moment when they hit on that sound in the dressing room of a Vancouver club.

"I played Billy this song and when we got to the chorus, he did the harmony above that. He got it. It sounded fantastic. It was a country tune, a pop tune. It was the Everly Brothers and Hank Williams and all these things together. I probably slapped him and said, 'This is exactly what it should sound like. Let's keep doing it!'"

As Hatcher stepped up his role in the group and the combo morphed from a Cowsill support band into a group entity of its own, the change in Cowsill's demeanor was notable. "He became Mr. Love after that. He started to turn on the charm. It became more of a two-frontman act. He was the golden voice and we were the harmonizing duo," says Hatcher.

With drummer Jay Johnson and Spanier on bass (later replaced by Barry Muir), it was obvious this could no longer be simply the Billy Cowsill Band. Always a fan of astronomy, Cowsill first offered up the name the Blue Stragglers, after a phenomenon defined by Wikipedia thusly: "The merger of two stars [which would] create a single star with larger mass, making it hotter and more luminous than stars of a similar age." Cowsill explained that blue stragglers were actually the reflected light of stars that had already died. "I thought that might be hitting a little too close to home," Chesney laughs. In the end, they settled on the Blue Shadows. Hatcher's partner Leah suggested the name, after the old Sons Of The Pioneers number "Blue Shadows On The Trail," which had become a favorite after Syd Straw's cover version on the Disney tribute album *Stay Awake.*

Onstage they evolved into a nimble, versatile outfit. Their sound hit some middle ground between hardscrabble country and chiming '60s pop. Covers included the Beatles' "Anytime At All," George Jones' "Hell Stays Open All Night," Canadian cult rocker Michel Pagliaro's "What The Hell I Got," and Joni Mitchell's "Raised On Robbery." When asked to define their style, they called it "Hank goes to the Cavern Club."

Alone at the microphone, Cowsill could summon a voice that brought to mind both Hank Williams and Roy Orbison. When Hatcher joined in, their voices locked and soared. The rudimentary rhythm section (including Cowsill's driving acoustic guitar) pumped like a piston as Hatcher coaxed simple, melodic, tremelo-laden melodies and stinging solos from his custom-made hollowbody guitar.

Hatcher and Cowsill began writing together, too, and their contrasts were complementary. If Cowsill was a zoom lens, instinctively drawing from a personal well of sadness or joy, Hatcher was wide-angled, looking for opportunities to transform those personal perspectives into something more universal. "Is Anybody Here" starts as a solipsistic cry from the heart, but by the end it converts into a broader social observation. Cowsill's seed for "Don't Expect A Reply" used the runaway train cliché to assert his badass stature; Hatcher used the later verses to comment on manifest destiny, linking hell-bent, personal destructiveness with the history of rapacious westward expansion: "I used to roll on through when it was countryside/Then the cities they grew until they reached the sky."

Their debut album *On The Floor Of Heaven* arrived in 1993, and it still sounds like it dropped from another era. The lead off track "Coming On Strong" erupts on a surge of sawing fiddles, Hatcher's chugging guitar and some sly wordplay. "When Will This Heartache End" could serve as a model for simplicity and elegance in pop songcraft. Hatcher resurrected his old Big Beat number "Deliver Me," and Cowsill's gravitas found new depth in the song.

Before the album's release, the group traveled to Nashville and played a showcase at 12th & Porter. "The band went onstage and it was the who's who of the music industry and they absolutely burned it to the ground," recalls Chesney. "If there was a moment I had where I thought things are about to change for us, that was it." Sony in Canada issued the album via co-manager Dave Wanagas' Bumstead Records, but a U.S. release remained elusive.

At South By Southwest in 1994, the response was equally enthusiastic. Cowsill and Hatcher were invited to perform at a later charity concert in Santa Monica in honor of the Everly Brothers. Amid a cast packed with heavyweights (including Dave Alvin and a taped performance by Brian Wilson), the pair performed a brief acoustic set that received a riotous response and the evening's only encore. They toured with The Band (which had reunited sans Robbie Robertson), appeared on TV in Canada, and garnered critical raves across the board.

And yet, no U.S. release. The Blue Shadows' tour T-shirts carried a motto: "Low Tech, High Torque." Modern country music, at the time infatuated with line dancing and New Country gloss, betrayed a different attitude: High Tech, Low Standards. Label personnel would tell Chesney that they loved the band and asked that he send them a copy when they did sign with a label. But none of those execs stepped forward to release it themselves. Says Chesney: "The resounding response [from Nashville] was: 'I love this band, but they scare me.'"

Still, there was enough promise and enthusiasm to take a run at a second album. Chesney still recalls in awe a day when Hatcher and Cowsill arrived at his Vancouver office to work up new material. As the manager walked by the pair to fetch coffee, Hatcher asked Cowsill what he'd been up to the night before. Cowsill mentioned he'd watched an old movie where someone used the phrase "my time's out of place." In the time it took Chesney to grab coffee and return, the duo had the song — a stately, moving ballad that would be a highlight of their sophomore effort — nearly completed.

Chesney was so energized by the song's potential, he couriered a cassette of the demo to friends, with no information on the tape case except these words: "Cadillacs for everybody!"

The Blue Shadows (clockwise from bottom left): J.D. Johnson, Barry Muir, Billy Cowsill, and Jeffrey Hatcher.

As the Blue Shadows moved ahead with work on their second record, something had changed with Cowsill. "We were kind of thrown together and it was expected of us that we would come up with equal weight in material, and he wasn't up to it," Hatcher reflects. "I used to say, 'What is the big deal if I bring in more songs? It'll be a co-write in the end. Relax about it.' He put a lot of pressure on himself, and that, with the emotional instability, produced a lot of canceled songwriting sessions."

Beyond songwriting, rehearsing became a chore. Then so did gigging. "He was fragile enough and difficult to work with," Hatcher says. "We all started to resent him. Every show was a fight right before, and every rehearsal he would pick a fight with somebody. So for months we couldn't learn a new song. It was professionally frustrating and irritating."

Hatcher pauses for a moment: "The poor guy is not here. I am trying to be objective; he is not here to speak for himself, but ultimately it is the way I saw it....Maybe I made him nervous.

and asked that he send them a copy when they did sign with a label.

I'm sure my darker side, when I would get irritated with him…he would not handle that well."

Associates of Cowsill confirm he was quietly abusing prescription medications and suffered bouts of bulimia. Cowsill hinted to Hatcher some darker issues in his past. "He had a lot of frustrations. There is a lot of pressure to be more and better and get bigger, and he hit the top young and got thrown down and came up with a lot of bruises,' he says. "My outsider's sense was Billy was not comfortable with things going well. He was unnerved by things not being in crisis all the time."

Arguments during the making of the second album became more intense. Cowsill falsely suspected Hatcher of sneaking extra songs onto the record. Relations began to frost over on the road, with Hatcher, Muir and Johnson remaining close, but growing distant from Cowsill, who would from time to time burst into tears in front of his bandmates. "I'm glad for him that he was able to do that because he needed a good cry," says Hatcher. "But it showed us how thin his resources were."

It all came to a bizarre head during a three-day layover in Ottawa. Hatcher looked out his hotel window and saw the group's van crashed halfway through a laundromat. Cowsill had gone to retrieve his guitar from the van, but somehow their vehicle shot across the parking lot and slammed through a brick wall. It was totaled. "I do not know how it happened," Hatcher says. "He didn't know. It was a complete mystery. And he came out unscathed. What the hell was he doing?"

Hatcher felt that matters were getting so out of hand, they should have scrubbed the second album, which came out in 1995 under the ironic title *Lucky To Me*. "I was so shattered by the craziness of that period that I could actually not hear," Hatcher says. "I must have given the thumbs up just to get out of the studio. Although I like parts of the second album, I feel divorced from it." The situation was dire enough that he suggested the Blue Shadows slam on the brakes to see if Cowsill could get right. "I said, 'We don't have to keep going. We can just stop playing. There is no law that says we have to keep playing.' Billy's answer was: 'I am in this for the long haul,'" Hatcher says.

The long haul was not much longer. And it was a haul. Hatcher went to management and declared: "We have to stop this train." And that was it. After a few contractual obligation gigs were dispensed with, the Blue Shadows were over. Cowsill briefly assembled a new Blue Shadows and played a brace of shows, but his condition deteriorated rapidly. Chesney learned Cowsill was drinking again, and the two old friends had a final confrontation that ended with the singer screaming at Chesney's back: "I was a good soldier!" With that last bridge burned, Cowsill bottomed out.

It may have ended there, but something miraculous happened. Against all odds, and with the help of his friend Neil MacGonigill (proprietor of the Calgary-based indie label Indelible Music), Cowsill turned his life around. He relocated to Calgary and got control of his demons. He put on weight and appeared healthy and happier than he had been in years. He worked with a new band, the Co-Dependents, released two albums, and became a guru to young musicians. And then just when he had his mental and spiritual house in order, fate delivered a cruel blow. He suffered Cushing's Syndrome (an overexposure to the hormone cortisol) and severe osteoporosis. Back surgery left him with a permanently collapsed lung, and the brittleness of his bones left him with two broken hips. Perhaps most harshly, he also developed emphysema, which required the use of an oxygen tank to breathe and made singing especially challenging. Then in early 2006, Billy received another blow. The body of his brother and Cowsills bandmate, bassist Barry Cowsill, had been recovered in New Orleans in the aftermath of Hurricane Katrina.

Chesney and Cowsill had by then buried the hatchet and were communicating by phone. During one call, Chesney remarked that his pal sounded especially chipper and asked why. "Hank wrote me a love letter," Cowsill replied, using a pet name for Hatcher. Hatcher's anger and disappointment at the Blue Shadows' failure had long ago subsided.

"I wrote to Bill to see how he was doing, but the spark for it was my hearing of his brother Barry's death. Bill and I had both performed for years with siblings, and I felt for him particularly because of that bond," Hatcher says. Cowsill phoned Hatcher to respond to the letter. The two spoke for about ten tearful minutes. "He sounded like he was on his way out. He sounded like he wasn't going to last much longer. It was a very sweet conversation," Hatcher recalls.

In February 2006, the very day Cowsill's family and friends were scattering Barry's ashes in their home state of Rhode Island, they received news of Billy Cowsill's passing.

"He was a diamond with many facets," says Chesney, who adds he used one of his final conversations with Cowsill to belatedly assure his friend: He was a good soldier.

These days, most of Hatcher's songwriting partners come from Winnipeg's inner city. His clients find their way to his makeshift music room through various means — trouble with the law, a reference by an allied therapist, a referral from social services organizations — but they tend to have something in common. "They need help over the fence. It's a big, complicated fence." Getting over the fence is achieved through hourlong sessions where, together, they will discuss an idea for a song, then work out what kind of melody or tone they are feeling (sad, angry, happy, hopeful). Over time they can progress to lyrics, different arrangements, different keys. All along, there is time to discuss how they feel about the exercise, to examine their own feelings and reactions.

"It can be any type of song. It can be something that is 20 minutes long and nothing is ever repeated. Or we can write a 30-second song where you just scream. We can stretch the boundaries," Hatcher explains. "You ask those questions all the time. Is this [song about] the past, present, where you want to go? Does it sound like a country road? Are there some bumps in it? You think there is danger in the ditches? We play that music and we go through that journey and we describe the journey. And if it is something they fear, how could we change it?

"Part of the fun for me is to take something that is second-nature for me, that musical facility that I have developed, and turning the therapy setting somewhat on its head, giving the client the chance to see their issue or their problem in a completely different way," he continues. "When they dig into themselves in a musical way, they are bound to come up with new points of view....Music is so universal, and it is so particular. Our experience is so universal and individual. You could spend your lifetime exploring both ends of that rainbow."

your lifetime exploring both ends of that rainbow." — Jeffrey Hatcher

When Hatcher reached his end of the rainbow with the Blue Shadows, he, Muir and Johnson pushed on for a time, joined by Wendy Bird. They played and recorded as the Sugar Beats (later the Reachers), and after the latter-day drama of the Blue Shadows, it was sweet relief to play for fun. But Hatcher concedes he did not foresee taking another serious run at mainstream success, and by the late '90s, he began casting around for a new direction.

"I didn't want to leave the field of music, but leaving the music business was fine with me. It had been such a head-butt for so long. While I still loved the music, the business got overwhelming and underwhelming. Irritating, to the point where I did not want to tackle it again. It would have involved finding management, finding a record label and rehearsing a band. And only one of those things is fun."

In the fall of 1996, Hatcher attended an open house at Capilano College in North Vancouver and learned that music therapy was, in fact, a serious discipline with lots of theory and proven results. It is not about volunteering to sit in the music room entertaining old folks or people in rehab or custody, although sometimes those noble activities are incorrectly described as music therapy. It is a true therapeutic discipline, and Hatcher enrolled in a Bachelor of Music Therapy degree program at the college.

Hatcher studied his prerequisites in English and Psychology, then music history, ear training, sight singing, piano, and more psychology. He undertook practicum placements in geriatric care, working with the elderly, but felt his metabolism still burned a little too high for that kind of work, so he found himself at the world-renowned Dr. Peter Centre. During his internship, he was hired as the center's music therapist. (The Dr. Peter

Jeffrey Hatcher with the Fuse, playing for fun in 2004. Photograph courtesy Stu Reid.

Centre, located in Vancouver, is named for Dr. Peter Jepson-Young, who was diagnosed in 1985 with HIV-AIDS. He gained notoriety for keeping an inspiring video diary during his illness, which was broadcast via the Canadian Broadcasting Corporation. The center which bears his name treats people who are challenged by HIV, addiction and/or mental illness. For more information, go to www.drpeter.org.)

Hatcher said the clientele there were 90 percent male (and half of the remaining percentage were transgendered male-to-female). All were HIV-positive. Some 70 percent were injection drug users. "If you scratch the surface, you find abuse, neglect, living on their own, prison history, learning disability. All those marginalized populations," he explains. "The issues we worked with were safe exploration of emotional life, music for relaxation and sometimes for pain management. Also it was a socialization tool. Many of my clients lived with intense isolation, from others and from their own emotional life. Communal music-making was an easy way to help bring them out of themselves by communicating non-verbally with others."

Hatcher provided to *No Depression* some of the songs produced in his work at the Dr. Peter Centre (with his clients' permission). The recordings are surprisingly sophisticated, with full-bodied arrangements in styles ranging from delta blues to softly pulsing disco. And the clients' voices, sometimes flattening or shaky, possess an audible sincerity and a desire to be heard.

Hatcher would occasionally organize coffee shop events at the center, and he invited his Sugar Beats bandmate Wendy Bird along to perform with him. "It was really rewarding to get together with Jeff because he is such a great person and any chance to play with him, I will take it," she says. "He is such a smart guy and such a sensitive soul, it made sense that he is doing that [music therapy]. I always thought it was very cool, that he could segue into that."

Hatcher expanded his education with a Master's degree in Counseling Psychology from Simon Fraser University in Vancouver; his thesis was titled *Therapeutic Songwriting With A Man Living With Complex Trauma*. In 2005, Hatcher and Decter returned to Winnipeg. A cluster of government-funded social service agencies, focused mostly on youth crime in the city, found the need for Hatcher's services in music therapy. It is, by most measures, making music in obscurity, but there's no question that Hatcher finds the work deeply rewarding.

Despite Hatcher's comfort outside the limelight, Wendy Bird has other plans. Her album of all-Hatcher compositions or co-writes, titled *Natural Wonder*, could spark some renewed interest in his work. The set was recorded in Vancouver, in a decidedly old-school style. Under the direction of the Odds' Craig Northey, a ten-piece band including members of the Odds and Vancouver's Barney Bentall & the Legendary Hearts recorded live in the studio. Half of Bird's vocals were done live, with some lush countrypolitan string arrangements added later. Bird called in some favors and worked her contacts to garner solos from Costello (who'd jammed with Hatcher some 30 years earlier in Winnipeg), guitar slinger Colin James, and Norah Jones' sideman Adam Levy. The ensemble took runs at some Blue Shadows numbers ("Don't Expect A Reply," "Is Anybody Here," "I Believe It"), some tunes dating to the Big Beat days ("In My Hand," "Deliver Me"), some unrecorded songs, and a brace from the never-released Sugar Beats album. Beyond confirming the odd lyric or chord, Hatcher had no involvement, which makes it particularly gratifying for the songwriter. "The fact that they liked it enough to do something with it is enough for me," he says.

Says Bird, who is exploring how to release the album: "We picked Jeff Hatcher because he is a good friend and writes such great songs. All the musicians who worked on the record know and loved those songs. It is my record, but it is a testament to Jeff's songwriting, too. It is a bit of a tribute to him."

All of this could be seen as evidence that, to paraphrase the Velvet Underground, despite all the amputation, music finds a way to survive. Hatcher points out that even nomadic cultures,

music therapy, Hatcher has quietly been making some new music of his own.

which carried only the essentials, packed instruments. Maybe those ancients knew something we've forgotten about how critical music is to our lives. And maybe it's why the best practitioners of music endure, alongside music.

Despite his ambivalence about the music business and his immersion in music therapy, Hatcher has quietly been making some new music of his own. Working once again with his brothers Don and Paul and his friend Dave Briggs, they have been picking away at some recent compositions. One of those new numbers, "What Yesterday Took," is built on a chiming twelve-string guitar figure and a gracious string arrangement, and it brings together insights from across his life in music:

> *And now you're on your own and nobody waits*
> *To dress or drive you*
> *And things so new jump out of corners at you*
> *None will survive you*
> *When you feel the ground is moving does the last time come to mind,*
> *When the aftershock was why the building shook?*
> *I hope tomorrow will bring back what yesterday took.*

Paul Cantin is a Toronto-based contributing editor and online columnist for No Depression. *He first saw Jeffrey Hatcher perform at a Winnipeg high school dance in 1977. Hatcher was later the subject of his 1987 Honors Journalism thesis, entitled* Trying Must Count For Something: An Odyssey In The Canadian Music Business.

I AIN'T MARCHING ANYMORE

IN PRAISE OF PHIL OCHS

by KENNETH J. BERNSTEIN

August 27, 1963, I was 17. That night I was in Greenwich Village preparing to head to Washington, D.C., for the civil rights march at which Martin Luther King Jr. would give his famous "I Have A Dream" speech. I had just graduated from high school, and had spent part of the summer active in civil rights demonstrations. I was staying the night with a friend, an African-American a bit older than me who I had met while picketing a hamburger chain that refused to hire blacks. We had to board the bus to D.C. early the next morning, but were too excited to sleep, so we went out to listen to speeches and music. That night I heard a man I knew nothing about, a man who had moved to the Village only a year before, singing this song:

William Worthy isn't worthy to enter our door
Went down to Cuba, he's not American anymore
But somehow it is strange to hear the State Department say
You are living in the free world, in the free world you must stay

SHOCKO GRAFIX, FROM AN A&M PROMOTIONAL PHOTOGRAPH

I was there that night because it seemed the focal point of people preparing for the forthcoming march. And Willie, the friend with whom I was staying, spent almost as much time in the Village as he did where he lived in Harlem, and more than on the picket line where we met. Why did this song so strike me? My political philosophy was still somewhat inchoate. I knew I was for civil rights, and had known it since I encountered segregated bathrooms in Miami on a family trip in December 1956. And I already had a visceral reaction to some of the right-wing expressions of the '50s, with perhaps my earliest political memory being the Army-McCarthy hearings. The last two lines of the chorus of that song somehow struck something in me — we were Americans, proud of our freedom, and yet afraid of it at the same time. The civil rights movement was an attempt to realize freedom for all at home. The words of Ochs pointed me at something broader, a set of implications I had not previously considered.

Of course I already knew of Woody Guthrie, and I had heard of Bob Dylan, Joan Baez, and Peter, Paul & Mary, knew about Pete Seeger and a few others. Indeed, in my own tentative attempts at playing guitar and singing, I often tried songs I associated with most of them. But who was this man whose words seemed so clearly to speak a simple truth? His lyrics grabbed my attention, especially that chorus.

I was not connected enough with musical circles to realize that Phil Ochs had already made an impression, both with appearances in and around New York, and earlier that summer in Rhode Island at the Newport Folk Festival. And for whatever reason, despite the undoubted gifts he had, both with lyrics and with music, he never broke through to a larger audience the way others did, even as his songs often spoke more directly to the issues at hand. But his words, his music, his singing touched me as much as anything written by Dylan or sung by Baez.

Phil Ochs, undated.

Never again was I to hear Ochs up close and live. And yet for quite a period his phrases would seem to speak to my condition, to my concern for the world in which I lived. Over the years, some of his songs have come to take on even more meaning: I hear them or again encounter the lyrics, and they can shock me out of complacency. For someone in his 60s as I am now, consider this final verse:

> *Once I was young and impulsive*
> *I wore every conceivable pin*
> *Even went to the socialist meetings*
> *Learned all the old union hymns*
> *But I've grown older and wiser*

because others performed his songs.

> *And that's why I'm turning you in*
> *So love me, love me, love me, I'm a liberal*

See the power of memory that is invoked, the challenge it raises? And how the challenge raised decades past is still applicable to those of us who, perhaps in arrogance, thought in our younger days that we would never succumb and become like those who he challenged in this song?

Of course, even before I really got to know Ochs, I knew Ochs, because others performed his songs. Joan Baez sang one that had a haunting effect upon me in college. Like many, I thought perhaps she had written it. Only much later did I realize its words were penned by Ochs:

> *Show me a prison, show me a jail,*
> *Show me a prisoner whose face has gone pale*
> *And I'll show you a young man with so many reasons why*
> *And there but for fortune, may go you or I*

Perhaps I should explain why that verse so affected me, even before I knew who had written it. I grew up in an upper-middle-class family, in a comfortable suburb. I had no direct experience of discrimination — our school system was about one-third Jewish — until a trip to Miami, where I first saw signs on bathrooms that said "whites only." That was in December 1956. The following fall our attention was directed to Little Rock, Arkansas, which for people of my generation meant that we saw directly how race divided this nation. As subsequent issues of civil rights were raised while I went through secondary school, I learned about those who put themselves at risk for things I took for granted.

I was also a troubled adolescent in a home dominated by problems caused by alcohol. For all the benefits of my upbringing and the supposed gifts I had, nurtured with private music lessons and even tutoring when I struggled with foreign languages, I was not that far removed from the kinds of catastrophes that place so many young people on destructive paths. I could easily have been arrested for more than a few of my juvenile escapades, but my family was connected enough that I never faced formal charges. And there, but for fortune…

Phil Ochs was a troubled soul whose career never fully matched his talents. He was, apparently, subject to depression in its bipolar form, and would eventually take his own life on April 9, 1976, when he was but 35. By then I had been through more than a few of my own troubles, troubles that at times had caused my family — and me — to wonder if I would ever amount to anything. I had had severe psychological problems in the late 1960s, including a period of hospitalization for my own depression. I dropped out of college three times before returning to Haverford College (near Philadelphia) in the fall of 1971; I finally finished the degree I'd begun working toward in 1963 when I graduated in May 1973. Along the way I had too many broken relationships, no real direction or purpose in my life. And even after graduating, I still struggled with a sense of purpose.

Through it all I remained committed to the idea of social justice. And even when I was not singing or playing the guitar, I continued to listen to songs that addressed social ills, and to try in whatever limited way I could to make a difference.

Phil Ochs was significant enough of a cultural figure to warrant a 600-word obituary in *The New York Times*. And yet his passing, like much of his musical effort, did not get the attention it deserved. Living in the Philadelphia area and not reading the *Times*, I was unaware of his death for several months. And even when I heard the news, when a friend was playing one of his albums at dinner and remarked about his suicide, I'm not sure I fully appreciated what we had all lost. Yes, Ochs felt frustrated that he could not longer produce songs as he had in the past, but the body of work was so immense, and so powerful.

Consider that he had co-written with Bob Gibson "Too Many Martyrs", a song with powerful images of Emmett Till and Medgar Evans, and so appropriate to the summer of 1963, when 250,000 of us came to Washington where men like Rev. Martin Luther King Jr. and John Lewis spoke, and the nation began to realize that it was not just Negroes who were concerned about what was happening. Think back to a time of Little Rock and Birmingham, of Freedom Rides and the bombing of synagogues, of marches and police riots, and then consider these words from the chorus of that song:

> *Too many martyrs and too many dead,*
> *Too many lies, too many empty words were said,*
> *Too many times for too many angry men,*
> *Oh, let it never be again.*

We often wonder about creative artists who die young, what else they might have produced. I often think of composers who lived briefly: Mozart was 35, Schubert 31, Purcell about 36, Bizet 36, and Arriaga ten days short of his 20th birthday. One cannot help but wonder what additional creative masterpieces we might now enjoy from the mind of each had they but lived longer.

Phil Ochs was not yet 36 when he took his life. Consumed with his own problems, he had not been particularly able to write about ours for a number of years before he passed. Thus perhaps it is a false path to wonder what else he might have written had he merely lived.

And if the problems that besieged him had been controlled? Think about this: Ochs was but a year older than Bob Dylan, who is still productive, although writing very differently from the young bard of the Village in the 1960s. The continued commentary that from time to time Dylan has offered in his songs is a role that might otherwise have fallen to Ochs, and given the power of what he did write, we can well wonder what else he might have offered us.

And clearly as we look at the absurdity of more than one administration in the three decades since Ochs passed, we can but imagine how his sharp wit could have skewered them as he did the political and other leaders of the time in which his writing was so potent. (Can you imagine "Here's To The State Of George W. Bush"?)

Still, rather than regret what he did not leave us, perhaps we can do something more important, which is to resurrect his words and music among a newer generation. Yes, some of his lyrics *might* seem dated by the time in which they first appeared, but is our time really so different from that about which Ochs wrote?

Perhaps I feel as strongly as I do because of my own life's journey. Despite my opposition to Vietnam and my participation in the civil rights movement, I found myself enlisting in the Marines in the mid-1960s — a decision I can assure you, having too belatedly become a Quaker, I would no longer make. At the time I believed I had an obligation to serve my country, and I did not want to foist my responsibility on those who lacked the ability, education or connections to find ways of avoiding military service. As it worked out, I only served Stateside, in data processing and in a military band, and I did gain GI Bill benefits that later enabled me both to finish college partially at government expense and to purchase the comfortable home from which I write this.

PHOTOGRAPH BY RON COBB/MICHAEL OCHS ARCHIVES

I was totally out of place in the military: I was opposed to the Vietnam War, yet I was in the Marines at the moment when American involvement in Vietnam was expanding. While I respect what I learned about myself in the Marines, I also acknowledge that the benefits may have been outweighed by my confusion — and by drinking, which was one of the forms of self-indulgent and destructive behavior in which I engaged to avoid confronting that confusion.

And yet throughout that time there was always music, although it must have seemed odd to my barracks-mates that this then clean-cut Marine would pull out his guitar and start singing anti-war songs, including words by Ochs. I suppose one could say this was a symptom of some of the personal problems that preceded (and perhaps led to) my enlistment, and which were to continue for some years after my discharge.

Ochs, too, was raised in the suburbs, by Jewish (though non-practicing) parents. His exposure to the military mind came earlier than did mine; the son of an Army doctor, he was educated at a Virginia prep school called Staunton Military Academy, and unlike many of his '60s compatriots, he never entirely lost his respect for men in uniform. Perhaps that is why some of the lyrics of Ochs' lesser-known songs speak to me. Take this, from "The Marines Have Landed On The Shores Of Santo Domingo", written about an event from that very time in the Johnson administration:

> *The crabs are crazy, they scuttle back and forth, the sand is burning*
> *And the fish take flight and scatter from the sight, their courses turning*
> *As the seagulls rest on the cold cannon nest, the sea is churning*
> *The Marines have landed on the shores of Santo Domingo*

Ochs opens and closes with those words. Let me offer another stanza, because it expresses as well as anything I have read or heard from Ochs the power of his ability to express the harsh reality to which too many blinded themselves:

> *Up and down the road, the generals drink a toast, the wheel is spinning*
> *And the cowards and the whores are peeking through the doors to see who's winning*
> *But the traitors will pretend that it's getting near the end, when it's beginning*
> *The Marines have landed on the shores of Santo Domingo*

Remember: I voluntarily served in the Marines. Like Ochs, I have a healthy respect for many who take that path, one I have not lost even as I eventually followed my heart and became a Quaker. Ochs' ability to criticize the way the military was used without necessarily damning the ordinary grunts is something that very much spoke to my soul.

The title of the piece you are reading, "I Ain't Marching Anymore," is from the pen of Phil Ochs, one of his best-known songs. The chorus goes like this:

> *It's always the old who lead us to the war*
> *It's always the young who fall*
> *Now look at all we've won with the saber and the gun*
> *Tell me is it worth it all*

Like many writers of that period, Ochs wrote powerfully and directly in opposition to a war he did not think had to be fought. In that sense, his words are as relevant today as they were in the 1960s, when many of my generation were saying in word and deed, "Hell, no! I won't go!"

As I write this, we may see one war winding down, but we must worry that the other — in Afghanistan — may soon expand. In the time of Vietnam, our young people were influenced by the voices of singers and songwriters. Some of those are still with us, people such as Baez and Dylan. For some reason, the voices in opposition to the wrongs of our time, including our involvement in wars of choice, have not spoken as powerfully as did those of the earlier time.

Phil Ochs, May 1965.

And perhaps too many of us have forgotten those voices, even as far too many never even learned that "And there but for fortune, may go you or I."

I have not forgotten Phil Ochs. From time to time I will play the one recording of him I still have, or I'll play records from that period and hear his music in the voice of others. I am thereby reminded of what I was like then, and how that period helped shape me into the adult I am now

in opposition to a war he did not think had to be fought.

— a Quaker, who chooses to try to make a difference by teaching social studies in a public school. Perhaps this piece can be my small part in reminding others of what Phil Ochs, in his far too brief life and even briefer career, gave us. And then perhaps we can all draw the line, as he did in his work, and stop careening toward ever more conflicts, by saying, as he sang:

I ain't marchin' anymore.

Peace?

Kenneth J. Bernstein is a teacher and writer, and a frequent blogger at dailykos.com.

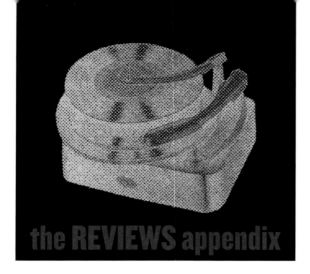

the REVIEWS appendix

TOGETHER AGAIN

BUDDY & JULIE MILLER
Written In Chalk
(New West)

by PETER BLACKSTOCK

WHEN NEWS began trickling out that the next Buddy Miller album — the first since 2004's widely acclaimed *Universal United House Of Prayer* — would in fact be a Buddy & Julie Miller album, it came as somewhat of a surprise, in a positive way. The married couple had not made a record bearing both their names since 2001's self-titled disc, and in recent years Julie has significantly retreated from the spotlight, rarely if ever appearing onstage. What's perhaps most striking, then, about *Written In Chalk* is that Buddy relies almost exclusively on Julie for the album's material. She's credited as the sole songwriter on eight of the disc's twelve cuts; one (the rollicking "Gasoline And Matches") is a Buddy/Julie co-write, with the other three being covers of songs from several decades past.

In a way, this makes perfect sense: De-spite not having issued a record of his own in nearly five years, Buddy has been plenty busy as a guitarist and producer. He finally took a break from Emmylou Harris' band last year in order to tour with Robert Plant & Alison Krauss, though he's also still doing occasional acoustic dates with Harris, Patty Griffin and Shawn Colvin (under the billing "Three Girls And Their Buddy"). In the studio, he's produced records for the likes of Solomon Burke, Allison Moorer and Jim Lauderdale, as well as contributing guitar and/or vocals to records by everyone from P.F. Sloan to Miranda Lambert to Rodney Crowell to Frank Black. Comparatively, Julie has had a bit more time than Buddy to focus specifically on songwriting.

At least one of these songs dates back to 2003, as it addresses the passing of June Carter Cash, who died in May of that year. Others were apparently written, or at least completed, much more recently, given the remarks Buddy made to *ND* co-editor Grant Alden about the album in the cover story of our final bimonthly issue in the spring of 2008: "She's been writing a ton of great songs, at least starting them and getting them halfway done…but she's finishing some of them."

In that interview, Buddy also alluded to the difficulties which led to Julie's retreat from performing, setbacks both physical (she suffers from fibromyalgia) and emotional (the death of her brother from a bolt of lightning). "I think out of this whole tough three or four years she's been able to put down some things," Buddy said. "And not all heavy stuff."

That last observation is essential to getting the full picture of this record. Despite the hard times that may have motivated Julie's writing, *Written In Chalk* isn't merely a litany of lament. Nowhere is that clearer than on the first track, "Ellis County," which may well be the best song Julie has ever written. At the very least, it's the most immediately appealing; by the second time you play it, you feel like you've known it all your life. The first verse begins with Buddy's voice singing her words of longing for a simpler era:

Take me back
When times were hard but we didn't
  know it
If we ate it, we had to grow it
Take me back
When all we could afford was laughter
And two mules instead of a tractor
Take me back again.

Julie joins in on the next verse, and the band (Larry Campbell on fiddle, Brady Blade on drums, Chris Donohue on bass, John Deaderick on keyboards) gradually builds up the song's upbeat country-folk-rock structure, using those traditional American sounds to celebrate the beauty of traditional American values. At a time when the future is collapsing under its own weight, there is warmth and wisdom in Julie's wishes and words: "Take me back."

A hint of her personal tragedy lurks within one line, as Julie pines for the days when "I had all my sisters and brothers." She digs deeper into that darkness on a trio of ballads where saying farewell, or trying to, is a recurring theme. On "Don't Say Goodbye," Patty Griffin sympathizes in harmony as she and Julie sing, "Take the stars down that I wished on/Take my tears so I don't cry." More elusive is "Everytime We Say Goodbye," which is bathed in sonic layers of guitar and keyboards.

The hardest hitter is the title track, an exquisite and dramatic number which features Griffin again, this time accompanying Buddy's lead vocal. "All I did was help you tell a lie/You never even knew it when I said goodbye," they sing, their voices wrung with desperation. And, vividly, in the lyric which gives the album its title: "All our words are written down in chalk/Out in the rain on the sidewalk." The way forward, finally, as has long been the case in Julie's music, as well as her life, is through her faith:

We don't know all the trouble we're in
We don't know how to get home again
Jesus come and save us from our sin.

A counterbalance is offered on "Smooth," a six-minute, down-and-dirty bluesy rocker about picking up a hitchhiker who has no particular place to go. Further diversity comes from the covers. "What You Gonna Do Leroy," a Mel Tillis tune covered by both Lefty Frizzell and Burl Ives, receives a subtle, swinging reading, as Buddy trades verses with Robert Plant. Things get turned up a few notches on the pop-soul nugget "One Part, Two Part" (written by Dee Ervin and recorded in the '60s by Clydie King), featuring a fiery vocal contribution from longtime Miller associate Regina McCrary. The album closes with Buddy and Emmylou Harris duetting on Leon Payne's "The Selfishness In Man," memorably recorded by George Jones

but coming across here as something Emmylou might have sung with Gram Parsons back in their brief collaborative heyday.

Preceding that track is the aforementioned song about the passing of June Carter Cash. Titled simply "June," it's the album's sparest and ultimately most moving moment, Julie's sweet whisper hanging just above Buddy's gently picked acoustic guitar strings and a faint touch of piano keys as she makes the bold move of stepping into Johnny Cash's shoes to empathize with his loss: "I know someday I'll sing with you again, but the love that you gave me will last until then." And there's the remembrance of how "the moon's face was hiding" on the ides of May in 2003, when "an eclipse of the moon said that you were gone."

The world misses June & Johnny to this day. But we've still got Julie & Buddy.

NEKO CASE
Middle Cyclone
(Anti-)

I T MAY SEEM like a prank at first that Neko Case has opted to close her fifth studio album with the sound of chirping crickets — 31 minutes and 39 seconds of the stuff, in fact. Titled "Dans Le Marais" (French for "in the marsh"), the track's generous helping of swampy actuality balloons the formal running time of *Middle Cyclone* past 73 minutes. It would be a joke on just about any other record, but it's hard to recall an artist who has become so utterly immersed in an infatuation with the natural world, and as such, the hissing of summer bogs is perfectly at home here.

The remaining 42 minutes and 13 seconds of more formal music infrequently strays from Case's focus on the animal kingdom and

the natural environment, and the barriers humans have constructed between those worlds. We're not talking about metaphors and pathetic fallacy here, though. When, in "People Got A Lot Of Nerve," Case adopts the voices of an unapologetic elephant and killer whale ("I'm a man-eater/But still you're surprised when I eat ya"), you're welcome to interpret it as an analogy for ill-advised human relationships. But it feels like Case is content to laud the instinctive integrity of animals — even ones with non-analogous sharp teeth.

Although it was made in Tucson, Toronto and Brooklyn, the heart of *Middle Cyclone* seems to be at Case's farm in Vermont, where some recording was done in her barn. Specifically, at the rural retreat she recorded a chorus of multiple pianos (all secured as giveaways from want ads), and the result is a uniquely rich but austere sound that beautifully serves the singer's most fully realized set of songs.

There were times that I tried
One for every glass of water that I spilled
* next to the bed*
Retching pennies in a boiling well
In a dream that at once becomes a
* foundry of mute and heavy bells*
They shake me deaf and dumb
Saying someone made a fool of me
For I could show them how it's done

That heady stream-of-consciousness verse, which comes from the title cut, is interrupted by a solo apparently played on a broken music box chime — a perfect complement to the lyric's bereft wordplay. "Can't give up acting tough," she sings. "It's all that I'm made of/Can't scrape together quite enough/To ride the bus to the outskirts of the fact that I need love." The brash, outward-looking songwriter of past records has, maybe in spite of herself, become an adroit confessional composer.

She's a smart cover artist, too. A waltzy, woozy cover of Harry Nilsson's "Don't Forget Me" and a clear-eyed run at Sparks' "Never Turn Your Back On Mother Earth" are perfectly of a piece, as unlikely as that might seem on paper. But then, when the principal instrument of interpretation is a voice as strong and distinctive as Case's, the pressure shifts off the material. On her own song, the brisk shuffle "This Tornado Loves You," there's a moment toward the end where she repeatedly invokes the title and then erupts with *"what will make you believe it"* in such a wrenchingly forceful way that you can't help but shake your head in wonder and reflect on a line from her song "I'm An Animal": "My courage is roaring like the sound of the sun."

Indeed. Neko Case is blessed with one of the great voices in contemporary pop music. The promise that has accumulated across her solo records and her numerous collaborations is emphatically delivered on *Middle Cyclone*.

— PAUL CANTIN

MADELEINE PEYROUX
Bare Bones
(Rounder)

WHEN MADELEINE Peyroux came out of left field, and the Left Bank, with her 1996 debut album *Dreamland* she was an anomaly: An American busker from Paris with an eerie connection to Billie Holiday, rendering coolly soothing versions of the country classics "Walking After Midnight" and "Lovesick Blues." The album drew raves, but as anomalies can do, Peyroux quickly faded from view.

There's no telling whether she would have faded back in had Norah Jones not altered the landscape for female pop singers with her massively successful 2002 album *Come Away With Me*. But when Peyroux belatedly returned in 2004 with *Careless Love*, featuring covers of Dylan, Leonard Cohen and Elliott Smith, she traded in her status as an anomaly to become one of the standard-bearers of a new, understated, jazz-inflected style that stood in stark opposition to the full-throated, melismatic, Mariah-derived emoting that was dominating the pop charts, not to mention "American Idol."

The question was whether this genre-crossing trend — which Cassandra Wilson's boldly eclectic mid-'90s albums played a big role in spawning — would last. On the two albums Jones has released under her name since *Come Away With Me*, she has largely been in a holding pattern. Newcomers including England's Corinne Bailey Rae and Katie Melua have enjoyed success in her footsteps without offering much that is original. But Peyroux, in following up her transitional 2006 effort *Half The Perfect World* (which split the difference between singer-songwriter covers and co-written originals), takes a decisive step forward with *Bare Bones*, a glowing set of songs on which she collaborated with Walter Becker and Joe Henry, among other established tunesmiths.

Like the elephant in the room, Peyroux's Billie-isms are impossible to ignore. But with her wide-ranging taste, intriguing personal narratives, eccentricities, and lack of vulnerability (which recalls Peggy Lee), Peyroux has gradually pulled away from Lady Day's influence. *Bare Bones*, a song-cycle about overcoming and even benefiting from loss — whether of a loved one, a home, a sense of direction, or a sense of place — offers the clearest look yet into her romantic but refreshingly unsentimental character, while maintaining her sense of mystery.

Having sung Charles Chaplin's mawkish "Smile" on *Half The Perfect World*, Peyroux offers the same prescription for overcoming misfortune here in a bouncy, guitar-strumming, almost Shirley-Temple-an mode: "Instead of feelin' low, get high on everything that you love/Instead of wastin' time, feel good 'bout what you're dreamin' of." The last thing people who are being laid low by the economy may want to be told is, "Instead of feeling broke/Buck up and get yourself in the black." And at a time of rampant foreclosures, I'm not sure how well "Homeless Happiness" will go over, either, in celebrating the singer's freedom from the rat race ("No hurries, no worries for me").

But Peyroux has become so comfortable in her own stylistic skin and in her own experience as a street survivor that both of those songs (written with Julian Coryell) break down any resistance. And when she intensifies her emotions on the lovely "I Must Be Saved" (which she wrote alone) and the haunting "Damn The Circumstances" (written with David Batteau and her regular producer Larry Klein), the force of her personality is something to behold. "Damn the circumstances/life is hard enough/Damn the bones that rattle/Faith is good enough," she sings, mixing Christian mysticism and bluesman's resolve.

Adorned by tidy organ fills, cello tones, tinkling electric piano lines and, on the pesky, metaphor-happy Becker collaboration "You Can't Do Me," soulful female backup singers, *Bare Bones* is anything but bare. But Peyroux's partnership with Klein thrives on a light touch. When she sings, "Without your love and treachery, the calm is all I feel," the music matches the sentiment. You can hear Joe Henry's stamp on "Love And Treachery" from three rooms away, but as his partner in noir, and as an artist with other kinds of stories to tell, Peyroux has the last word.　— LLOYD SACHS

DAVID BYRNE & BRIAN ENO
Everything That Happens Will Happen Today
(Todo Mundo)

UNLESS YOU'RE Winnie-the-Pooh, the Buddha, or a newborn baby — i.e., an uncarved block — it's unlikely you've come to *Everything That Happens Will Happen Today* free of preconceived notions. Yes, 27 years have passed since David Byrne and Brian Eno's last album as co-writers, 1981's *My Life In The Bush Of Ghosts*, but the repercussions of that masterpiece still resonate powerfully. From early hip-hop to the vanguard of contemporary dance rock, down to all the crappy global fusion grooves wafting through expensive hotel lobbies, their revolutionary mish-mash of found sounds and unconventional rhythm remains a Rosetta Stone for contemporary music.

Yet lest we forget, the circumstances surrounding *Bush Of Ghosts* were very different. It was forged in the crucible of an intense ongoing relationship between the two individuals, which had started with Eno's chugging homage to Talking Heads, "King's Lead Hat," in 1977. The Heads made three albums in rapid succession with Eno behind the controls, culminating in 1980's *Remain In Light*, which (with a little help from MTV) pushed Byrne and his cohorts as close to the mainstream as they'd gotten to date.

In marked contrast, *Everything That Happens* came together much more casually. While working on the 25th-anniversary reissue of *Bush Of Ghosts*, the reluctant lyricist Eno revealed he had a clutch of unfinished musical sketches that might amount to something more, and Byrne offered to try his hand at concocting words and melodies. It was that simple. Their reunion may have sparked abundant hoopla among the media and fans, but its product is surprisingly, even deceptively, mellow.

The first teaser made public was "Strange Overtones," offered as a free download in advance of the album. A chunky yet fluid soup of burbling beats and multi-tracked vocals, it seemed to hint at the artists' awareness of their precarious position: "This groove is out of fashion/These beats are twenty years old," sang Byrne. Second thoughts, gentlemen?

No. Because the finished full-length exists in an entirely different universe from *Bush Of Ghosts*. If "Strange Overtones" is a bridge between the two records, so are Talking Heads' "This Must Be the Place (Naive Melody)" from 1983's *Speaking In Tongues* and the rough-hewn highlights of *Little Creatures* and *True Stories*. The opener of *Everything That Happens*, "Home," chugs along like a cartoon jalopy, with Byrne keening in his nasal twang behind the steering wheel; harmonically, the song recalls such established classics as "Save The Last Dance For Me" and "The Sounds Of Silence." It's instantly familiar.

That particular tune is a much more accurate reflection of the overall character of *Everything That Happens*. This folksy program offers an alternate, but accessible, vision of America, a la the Magnetic Fields' country-tinged 1994 full-length *The Charm Of The Highway Strip*. Listen to how Byrne's laundry-list lyric ("Japanese chairs in somebody's concert/Telephone bills on the company paycheck")

and off-the-cuff delivery tacks down the skittering, kitten-on-the-keys piano parts of "I Feel My Stuff." The pieces might seem incongruous, but they snap securely together. This is IKEA Americana, functional and no-frills, yet vibrantly colored, and boasting broad appeal.

Both men have paid lip service to the influence of gospel on these songs. A longshot? Not necessarily. After all, "Slippery People" was a club hit for the Staple Singers, and Bono did his best to touch the face of God on U2's Eno-produced classics *The Unforgettable Fire* and *The Joshua Tree*. The imagery of this album's final cut, "The Lighthouse," touches on familiar gospel tropes (seeking shelter, looking for one's place in the vast natural world), yet the real commonality is not one of words or timbres, but of intention: *Everything That Happens* sounds open, honest, and unfussy, more down-home than high art.

— KURT B. REIGHLEY

BRUCE ROBISON
His Greatest
(Premium)

DURING MY three decades of scamming my living as a rock critic (a career option that these days has all but disappeared), the most common misperception I encountered is that music journalists are really frustrated musicians. Jealous, even. A variation on a cliché: Those who can, do; those who can't, critique.

Au contraire, gentle reader. There are few musicians with whom I'd even consider exchanging my life (and then only if my wife Maria and my daughters Kelly and Molly could come with me). Any journalist who has spent much time in the musical trenches knows just how boring are those endless hours at soundcheck, in the recording studio, at the motel, in the van (or on the bus, for the marginally more fortunate). When I lived in Austin, I knew many musicians who loved living there so much that they spent 75 percent or more of their time on the road just to pay the bills back at the home they so rarely saw.

Meanwhile, I slept in my own bed, had dinner with my family, and enjoyed the perks of a health plan, paid vacations and regular salary. Jealous of musicians? I'd as likely be jealous of gypsies.

But if I were a musician, one whose career I'd aspire to emulate would be Bruce Robison's. I know him only as a passing acquaintance from those Austin days, but I feel I know him a whole lot better from the decisions he's made, and even more from the songs he writes. He seems like a man of common-sense decency, whose priorities are more personal than the priorities of the music industry, and who writes songs that obviously mean a lot to him but have somehow become huge hits for the likes of George Strait, the Dixie Chicks, and Tim McGraw & Faith Hill.

Where others might scheme or sell their souls to the devil — or at least Music Row — to enjoy the success as a songwriter that Robison has, he's done it by being Bruce Robison, just a regular guy. It's like he won the lottery. (No gratuitous Kelly Willis reference here.)

Among the ten songs newly recorded for this compilation, some of them are Robison's most popular ("Travelin' Soldier"), some of them are his most personal ("My Brother And Me"), and some of them are both ("Angry All the Time," "Desperately," "Wrapped"). Most of them are recorded here by Robison for the second or third time, following his self-titled indie

release in 1996 (heard by few outside Austin), and later on his pair of albums for the major-label subsidiary Lucky Dog. He asked for his release from that label because neither the bigger production nor the incessant touring required for promotion suited his style.

The new recordings reflect the listener's familiarity with the hit arrangements, but they also reflect Robison's maturation over the last couple of decades. Songs he wrote when he was a lovesick troubadour in his 20s he now sings as a long-married father of four. He accepts the reality that he isn't as dynamic a performer as his older brother (Charlie, credited in the notes as "my hero") and that he lacks the vocal chops of his wife (the aforementioned Willis, who provides harmonies and is credited in the notes as "the love of my life…who inspired many of these songs").

Yet it's hard to imagine a singer who sounds more comfortable in his own skin, with nods toward the conversational phrasing of James Taylor and the understated delivery of Don Williams. Ultimately, *His Greatest* feels like the end of a chapter, with the release last fall of the aptly titled *The New World* launching chapter two.   — DON MCLEESE

VARIOUS ARTISTS
Keep Your Soul: A Tribute To Doug Sahm
(Vanguard)

IT'S BEEN almost ten years since Doug Sahm checked out of the motel, and the silence in his absence has been deafening. He left no real protégés, no treasure trove of unreleased studio recordings, no live recordings of him throwing out his captivating mix of Texas blues, Texas country, Texas soul, and Texas Tex-Mex to 200 hippies jammed into

Soap Creek Saloon, from his hits "She's About A Mover" and "Mendocino" to obscure originals (meaning almost every other song Doug wrote), along with exotic covers of Dylan, Jagger, Sunny Ozuna and Jimmy Donley, among others.

Tribute albums are so common that the concept has been trivialized, but in the case of Douglas Wayne Sahm, son of San Antonio and the easily the most genuine multitalented Texas musician ever — no shit, think about it, who else could pass for black, brown, white and Cajun like Doug did, and play guitar, steel, or fiddle with equal authenticity? — *Keep Your Soul: A Tribute To Doug Sahm* is the finest testament to Doug yet. Conceived by sonicboomers.com executive editor Bill Bentley, who put together a superfine Roky Erickson tribute when he was at Warner Bros., *Keep Your Soul* keeps the flame burning with a suitably eclectic collection of Dougheads who resuscitate his soul and spirit.

Ry Cooder with Little Willie G singing lead gets the party started with an unconventional, thoroughly infectious East Los Angeles reading of "She's About A Mover," the 1966 pop hit that put the Sir Douglas Quintet on the map. Los Lobos follow by staying faithful to the original version of "Didn't Even Bring Me Down," capturing the tune's horn/guitar/B3 Chicano R&B groove. Santone-born, SoCal-bred Alejandro Escovedo, who got to Austin a decade after Doug did, goes straight for the guitar jugular on "Too Little Too Late," thankfully minus Doug's abuse of phase shifters. Stripping off the gloss to reveal the song's raw sentiment, Al translates Doug like he was Dylan, which would have pleased the old man to no end.

Greg Dulli's twang take on "You Was For Real" is a dark piece of cosmic cowboy wisdom in a Gram Parsons kinda way that recalls the tough time Doug had adjusting to "the purple hair crowd," as he called the punk/new-wave generation. He shouldn't have fretted because Dulli illustrates how Doug's songcraft spoke to the grunge scene. Dave Alvin hits a similar country note on "Dynamite Woman," probably the best-crafted pop song by Doug that wasn't a hit, with sparkling steel riffs that recall Waylon Jennings' "Rainy Day Woman" more than Doug's own sound.

Then Flaco Jimenez y su conjunto backed by the Westside Horns bring Doug back to life with "Ta Bueno Compadre," a jaunty bilingual polka that is payback for Doug exposing Flaco to the greater music world beyond San Antonio. It's like he's back *en el West Side*, hanging with his compadres all over again.

Delbert McClinton's "sanging" on "Texas Me" and Terry Allen's "playin'" on "I'm Not That Kat Anymore," the latter featuring Joel Guzman on accordion and Lloyd Maines on pedal steel, celebrate the rarely appreciated Lubbock-San Antonio musical dynamic. Jimmie Vaughan's reading of Doug's '50s-vintage teen lament "Why Why Why" celebrates Doug's bluesier tendencies. Vaughan's fretwork is down and dirty, with sour-key horn bleats as counterbalance, but it's his wailing vocal that flatters the original by oozing the kind of greasy teen sentiment drenched in echo that all great rock 'n' roll records once possessed.

Charlie Sexton and the Mystic Knights of the Sea (Mike Buck, Will Sexton, John Reed, Speedy Sparks) zone in on "Doin' It Too Hard," a track from *Rough Edges*, the 1973 compilation of outtakes that Mercury issued to capitalize on Jerry Wexler's *Doug Sahm And Band* album for Atlantic. Charlie showcases Doug at his most stoned, fuzzed-out rock 'n' roll indulgent, with a hint of a psychedelic jam emerging from the James Brown-worthy catatonic chant, "You're doing your thing too hard, little girl, you're doing it much too hard..."

The Gourds glorify the lost tradition of a border run to hang out til dawn in Boys Town with an intoxicating cover of "Nuevo Laredo." The country two-stepper "Be Real" pulls together most of Freda & the Firedogs (Doug collaborator Tommy Detamore replacing David Cook on pedal steel), a reminder that Marcia Ball sang country before becoming a blues queen, and that the Firedogs were frequent collaborators with Doug in early '70s Austin before anyone heard of Austin.

Joe "King" Carrasco's revved-up reading of the forgotten barnburner "Adios Mexico," a Doug song about girls and Mexico, is easily the album's jumpiest Tex-Mex rocker. Doug's son Shawn and Doug's sidekick Augie Meyer close things out by eerily reviving "Mendo-cino," note-for-note. Shawn proves he's a chip off the old block with his sound-alike vocals and his tendency to turn up the guitar loud enough to drown out everyone else, with Augie's signature Vox organ taking me back to the roller rink.

Meaning, this is a great thing, especially if you missed Doug the first time around. It makes me hope for a second album of tributes featuring Dylan, Willie, Asleep At The Wheel, Calexico, Sunny Ozuna, the Creedence rhythm section of Stu Cook and Doug Clifford, Jim Dickinson, Raul Malo, Alvin Crow, Max Baca and Texmaniacs, Little Joe Hernandez, Homer Henderson, the Krayolas, Levon Helm, Boz Scaggs, Ian Hunter, Cracker, ZZ Top and Roky Erickson.

But for an old Doughead like me, *Keep Your Soul* is bittersweet. The music is so good, it reminds me how big the hole in my soul has grown now that the real deal is no longer around. Thanks, Doug, for all the beautiful vibrations. — JOE NICK PATOSKI